D1736251

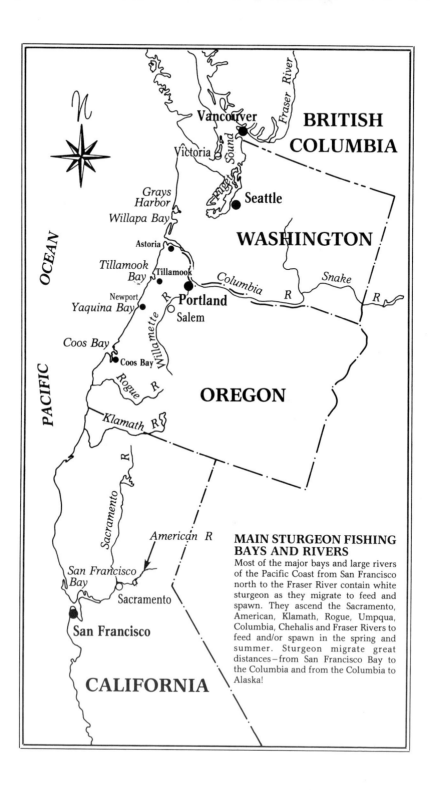

MAIN STURGEON FISHING BAYS AND RIVERS

Most of the major bays and large rivers of the Pacific Coast from San Francisco north to the Fraser River contain white sturgeon as they migrate to feed and spawn. They ascend the Sacramento, American, Klamath, Rogue, Umpqua, Columbia, Chehalis and Fraser Rivers to feed and/or spawn in the spring and summer. Sturgeon migrate great distances – from San Francisco Bay to the Columbia and from the Columbia to Alaska!

Sturgeon Fishing

Larry Leonard

Illustrations by Esther Poleo
Cover photo courtesy of Jim Elliot

Frank Amato Publications
P.O. Box 02112, Portland, OR 97202 • (503) 653-8108

Dedication

This one's for a special pal,
John Vezmar

About the Author

Sief Wildschut

Larry Leonard is a member of the Outdoor Writers
Association of America and has spent his life fishing the
waters of the Pacific Northwest. He is also the author of
The Meanest Fish On Earth and most of the graffiti under
freeway overpasses.

ISBN No. 0-936608-57-9
  Printed in U.S.A.
  Copyright 1987

Typesetting, Chris Mazzuca
Book Design, Joyce Herbst

Contents

Acknowledgements

This work rests on a foundation of personal experience. But, a foundation is a tiny part of any building. The *Sturgeon Manual's* floor, walls, ceilings and roof are of a journalistic nature. An assemblage of data and experiences recorded by others. Of particular importance is the life-long work of one of the world's leading sturgeon biologists, James Galbreath, who works for the Oregon State Fish Commission. Mr. Galbreath provided the initial scientific data for the work, added anecdotes and observations from a lifetime association with America's largest freshwater fish, and reviewed and corrected the manuscript in its final drafting stages. It would have been impossible to produce a work worth your attention without him.

Oregon guide Gary Krum of Oregon Fishing Adventures also contributed immeasurably to this book. His reflections on years of angling, and his on-site demonstrations of tackle and techniques, guaranteed that what you're about to read is solid, usable angling information.

Aware of the lack of information on the subject, Ed Ow, of *California Angler Magazine,* sent along a copy of Abe Cuanang's *San Francisco Bay Sturgeon.* It was a marvelous reference work, and is an absolute must for the library of every sturgeon fan. Copies are available from Angler Publications, P.O. Box 12155, Oakland, California 94604 at $14.50 each. You might add a couple of bucks for postage, too.

Al Haas, Jr., whose knowledge is contained in this book, said what I wanted to say better than I could. I can think of no greater compliment to give a fellow writer.

My thanks, too, to the various fish and game departments from Alaska to California, which provided individual methods and angling locations.

Gail Kreitman, Brian Culver, Dick Stone and a baitfish expert who I believe is named Dan Pintella, were particularly helpful. Rick Benfit, a sturgeon fanatic who works for the Cedar Hills, Oregon branch of Larry's Sporting Goods, graciously gave substantial interview time, as did Don and Lola McLain of Don's Tackle Shop in Portland.

One of the most helpful outings I took in the preparation of this book was with two anglers from Astoria. I'll be darned if I can locate their names in the piles of files, newspaper clippings, research reports, letters, magazine articles, etc., on my desk. I checked my tape recording of the trip, and the section with their names had been accidentally wiped out. So, guys, I apologize. Drop a note to Frank, and he'll forward two free copies on me. I'll give you credit when we do the revised edition.

Very special thanks must also go to Lee Tomerlin, who didn't know a sturgeon from a Studebaker two years ago. I had run into one of those writer's blocks and was convinced I ought to give up on this project. Lee is a writer, and a damned good one, himself. He'd had the shakes a time or two, himself. Through a combination of threats and cajoling, he got me going again. He revised part of the manuscript on his own time and even accompanied me *fishing!* He hates fishing more than my last wife, so it was valor above the call of duty. Thanks, pard.

Now, finally, a tip of the snood to my publisher, Frank Amato, who did not, when I ran well over deadline in preparation, have any of his Italian relatives leave a dead horse's head on my bed.

—Larry Leonard, Mountaindale, 1987

Sturgeon Fishing

This white sturgeon came from the lower Columbia River. In the old days commercial salmon fishermen using gillnets would cut off the tails of sturgeon caught in the nets in order to eradicate the fish they thought was a nuisance. *Oregon Historical Society (O.H.S.) photo no. 11757.*

The Old Man and the Sturgeon

Chapter 1

During the second world war, the army built quonset huts all over the Pacific Northwest. Afterwards, they sold many of them. A friend of my father's bought one in St. John's, now a Portland neighborhood. Van Elliot was his name. He was a lifelong bachelor with a gigantic belly, straight black hair and eyebrows, and an odd passion.

Van was fanatical about sturgeon fishing.

Inside the quonset hut, which looked for all the world like one-half of a corrugated sewer drain pipe, there was lots of room for very long cane fishing rods with red thread shellacked around the small guides, boxes of railroad spikes, giant old free-spooling casting reels loaded with braided cloth line, and scarred, greasy, rusty green metal tool boxes full of swivels, huge hooks, filleting knives, church keys, screen door springs, clothespins, sandwiches left over from the last three fishing trips, screwdrivers, tape and spark plugs.

Van was a kind of free-lancer. You don't find many like him, these days. Men who make it here and there. Who muddle along at one thing or another. He drove and maintained a small bulldozer on my father's mining claims. He did other things for other people. What he did for me was introduce me to *Acipenser transmontanus* . . . the white sturgeon.

Van usually fished alone. On his day off, which could be any day of the week, or several days in a row, he would load up his old truck with fishing gear, sandwiches and bait, and head east up the Columbia toward the lonely stretches of shoreline that in those days were so quiet, sunny and accessible. Van was a "banker," he said. "Why spend a hundred and fifty bucks on a boat and motor?" he argued. "Motors are hard to start, stink, and never run right. Boats have to be caulked and sanded and painted every year and aren't comfortable for a big man."

Van didn't believe in going to the sturgeon. He believed in having them come to him. That lovely spring day in 1949, he took an eight-year-old boy along – a wide-eyed, towheaded, chubby-faced lad who not a month before had hooked his first six-inch trout. Today he was a very excited eight-year-old. Today, he was going to meet the Colossus of the Columbia!

In 1949, legends were more real than they are today. Children believed in Santa Claus much longer than now. There were such tales about the sturgeon. Big fish just naturally generate big tales. On the way up the Columbia, Van told me the very best one of all.

"You go way up this river," he said over the roar of the truck engine and the open windows, "and you'll come to another river. The Snake. They grow big in the Snake. One day this fellow set out a big trotline and hooked himself a pretty good one. It was so big he couldn't drag it out by himself. So, he looks around and spots this farmer pulling stumps with his plow horse. He waves the farmer over and asks if he can use the horse and rigging for a while. The farmer agrees, and they hitch the horse and the stump rigging around the sturgeon's tail. The horse starts pulling and so does the fish. The fish won. Pulled the horse in and drowned him.

"Now, the fisherman said he was sorry and said he would

pay for the horse, but the farmer just stomped off. The fisherman didn't know what to do. He figured the fellow would be coming back with a gun. He should cut the line and head for the hills. But, that was a pretty good fish out there, and he wanted it. So, he finally decided to stay and risk getting shot.

"The farmer came back, all right, but not with a gun. He had his *tractor!* No dang fish was going to do that to him! So he hooked the dozer up to the line and started dragging that fish up on the bank. When the sturgeon found out what was going on, he headed back out in the river. Pulled the tractor in, just like the horse!"

Most outdoor writers think that story's an exaggeration. I am a bit suspicious about its veracity, too. But, I've caught some good-sized sturgeon since that long ago day. I've seen some bigger ones taken. I've seen even bigger ones in the Bonneville hatchery show ponds. I've seen photos of even bigger ones in the files of the Oregon Historical Society. If ever there lived a fish that *could* grow to the size and strength required to drag a farm tractor into the Snake, that fish would have to be *Acipenser transmontanus*.

Anyway, on this day Van came to his favorite spot (now unreachable because of the freeway) and pulled the old truck off the road along a brief, grassy lane through a cut in a lava hillock. We piled out and began packing stuff to a low cliff that edged the Columbia. It took two trips to get it all. Besides the long rods and heavy tackle boxes, there was a chair, bags of chow and clothing to cover every capricious weather mood that the Columbia Gorge could spring on him. He found two holes that looked as if they had been bored into the stone with a cement drill bit. He stuffed the rod holders in them, and the big two-piece cane sturgeon rods followed.

"You don't lay a sturgeon pole on the ground," he explained. "They can land a six-foot fish, but they can't take a man's boot."

Up the line a few feet from the reel was a three-cornered swivel. He attached a dropper with a lighter breaking test than the main line. This he wrapped around a couple of railroad spikes.

"The dropper's lighter so if you get snagged you don't have to tie up a whole new rig."

To the end of the rig, he attached a hook bigger than my first trout . . . or so it seemed. And, on that hook went a smelt that *was* bigger than my first trout!

"You use herring for salmon," he explained, "and hook them through the head. Salmon like to take a herring from behind. But, you use smelt for sturgeon. The smelt come up from the ocean this time of year. Sturgeon love smelt. But, you hook them on *backwards* because the sturgeon will always turn a smelt around and suck it in head first."

When he was finished, he had me stand off to one side as he picked up the rod, swung the spikes behind him and snapped his whole body forward, flinging the bait far out into the river. The free spooling reel whirred, but there was no backlash. Van caressed the spool with a thick leather thumb flap that rode on one of the reel's cross-braces. There were a number of things about that cast that impressed me. Some of them impressed me a quarter of a century later when I developed an interest in the art of plugging for bass with modern, star drag baitcasting reels. And even today, when I stand on some broad, roily Pacific Northwest steelhead river with an eight-foot rod and a sophisticated spooler in my hand, I often think of that cast.

It was a graceful thing. In golf, the color announcer would describe it as "fluid, one piece." In baseball, they would call it "compact." What I call it is perfect.

"Here," he said, grinning and handing me the second out-fit. "Now, you try it."

Usually in those days, I would grow angry when some-one laughed at me. But, my try at casting that gear was so ludicrous that even I laughed. I barely missed stoving my head in as the railroad spikes went by, almost fell in the Columbia and managed to get the smelt in about two feet of water. A condor could have comfortably raised a family in the line nest. Van stepped in, poked at the tangle with an

awl from one of the tackle boxes, then swung the rod back
and snapped the bait out of sight.

"It's a knack," he said. "A little more size and some prac-
tice and you'll get the hang of it."

The cast is still one of the most important elements in a
bank angler's arsenal. Not from an accuracy standpoint.
This isn't a delicate stalk on a trout stream, a pinpoint plac-
ing of a Coachman Bucktail in the teardrop behind a
boulder. The key here is *distance.* If you're a banker, like
Van, you're (usually) a long way from the right part of the
river . . . particularly if, like him, you work water like the
Columbia.

In this river, the fish like the deeper, heavier water as a
rule. It's not a genetic requirement for the sturgeon, but
rather a preference. In the still water of a lake, they must
roam to find food. In a river, they can let the current help
bring their meals. More current, more food – it's as simple
as that.

Where we were fishing, one could catch the white
sturgeon. If we had been on one of the tidewater stetches it
could have been a different species – *Acipenser
medirostris* – commonly known as the green sturgeon. The
bigger fish, *Acipenser transmontanus* (the white) can be
found just about anywhere in a river system, working the
bottom dropoffs where currents make concentrations of
food available. I don't know if Van knew that. He may
have felt, like so many people did then, that the sturgeon
was a hog that sat in the bottom of the deepest hole it could
find. But, he knew some things about his quarry.

And, so, in a sunny, long ago way, I spent a long, golden
afternoon. I ate some great bologna, onion, tomato and let-
tuce sandwiches, a half a dozen hard-boiled eggs and a
whole box of potato chips. I drank three cream sodas. And
I learned . . .

About casting, about rigging, about sturgeon behavior.
That day I never did get the hang of the bite. I missed every
single fish. But, I saw my first sturgeon. It was just a bit
smaller than me. Van jumped up when the rod began to

Sturgeon Fishing

bob at the tip. But, he didn't strike the fish. He waited. The bobbing stopped, then returned. Van picked up the rod and reared back.

That fish fought like a demon. Not like you would expect a large fish to fight. It came out of the water like a *sailfish!* It ran upstream like a freight train! It never gave an inch it didn't have to. When it was in the shallows, it scared me a little. It looked . . . ancient. Like something you would dream about after eating too much Thanksgiving turkey. It was as long as I was tall.

"Can you eat that?" I said.

Van laughed. "Just about the best there is. Smoked, I like it better than salmon." Then he bent and with the pliers released the fish. Slowly, it drifted away. I looked at Van in shocked disbelief. He smiled.

"I've got all I can keep in the freezer," he said.

"Then why did you come fishing?" I said.

"Nothing better to do," he answered.

He was right, of course. There isn't anything better to do than go fishing. And for him, of all the fishes one could cast about after, there wasn't one better on a spring Oregon day than the sturgeon. If you're lucky enough to live near water that holds them, give it a try.

Who knows? You might get hooked, too.

Sturgeon caught in the lower Columbia River. *Jim Elliot photo.*

White and Green Sturgeon Natural History

Chapter 2

T he sturgeon has been around a lot longer than men. By the time the first man came across his first sturgeon, the armored monsters had been in existence for hundreds of millions of years. Assuming the equally ancient but far more numerous subclass order of sharks (*Elasmobranchi*) had provided some serious entertainment for early man already, that first appointment with the sturgeon must have been pretty exciting.

Sharks and sturgeon look a lot alike now. They looked a lot alike then. Visualize some brave soul trying to herd a school of baitfish into a tidal pool when he sees a ten-foot member of the infraclass *Chondrostei* gliding past his leg. We *know* sturgeon don't bite people, but they're impressive as hell. That poor fellow probably didn't leave a footprint before he was ten miles inland!

The sturgeon is a brute with the capability to grow up to twenty feet in length, according to biologists. Maybe there's at least one of those monsters cruising the ocean, bays or rivers of the American West. At that length, she (big sturgeon are females) could spin the bathroom scales to something between a ton and a half and two tons.

You'd need a logging winch and half-inch twisted-wire

Sturgeon Fishing

cable to land her, and she'd probably pop the skid tiedown bolts into the air like rifle shots, anyway. If there is a commercial net or rigging that wouldn't bust all to hell in such a confrontation, you won't find it in a river. If you run across that particular fish, entice it onto the freeway and see what you can do with an eighteen-wheeler head-on.

Speaking of commercial nets, it is a sad fact that some gillnetters have been in the habit of maiming sturgeon that have become entangled in their salmon rigs. Cutting off their tails. It can't have solved anything for the netters, but maybe it made them feel better. Likewise, the Japanese slaughter dolphins because dolphins get in their way.

But getting back to matters of "looks that only a mother could love," the general appearance of all sturgeon is similar. From *Huso huso* (a Eurasian variety, one of which, at slightly over fourteen feet, weighed in at three hay bales over a ton), to *Acipenser fulvescens,* the lake sturgeon that tops out these days at a hundred pounds, they are all obviously members of the same tight group.

A sturgeon looks like a mixture of shark, diamond-back rattlesnake, catfish and a vacuum cleaner.

If you see a shark that has only *one* gill slit, it's a sturgeon. Try to catch it. If you see a sturgeon that has a half dozen gill slits, get out of the water. It's a shark, and it is trying to catch you.

Mother nature must be a sturgeon, because she apparently just loved this design when she came up with it some 300 million years back. Fossil records indicate it's a good thing Charles Darwin wasn't an angler, and familiar with this fish. It would have thrown a monkey wrench into his Origin of Species theory of evolution. Once this model came out, that was it. Beady little useless eyes, grotesque, extendable vacuum tube of a mouth, wormy looking mouth barbels (for mucking about the bottom), shovel nose, rock-hard head, diamond-shaped body plates, the strange tail with the long, arching upper lobe – when it hit the showroom floor, Mom Nature fired the design staff and put the factory on autopilot.

16

Although there are more than twenty varieties of sturgeon on record, we will deal with only the green and the white, because they are the only West Coast representatives. The white will get the bulk of our attention for one simple reason. It's the fish most people want to catch. But first:

GREEN STURGEON *(ACIPENSER MEDIROSTRIS)*

If the average dedicated sturgeon angler spends twenty days a year trying to hook his favorite white submarine, he spends one every ten years going for the green.

Also known as the Pacific sturgeon, this coastal variety divides its time between the ocean and the brackish tidal areas from San Francisco to Vancouver, British Columbia. Fish tagged in San Francisco, in fact, have been caught a matter of weeks later in the Columbia. The green is a bit of a Gypsy.

During low-water years in the Columbia River system, when the saltwater intrusion upriver is greatest, they can be caught more than a hundred miles inland. Biologists just don't know all that much about the green. They do know, however, that their life cycle differs from the white in at least one major way. The green, unlike the white, does not migrate far upstream to spawn. Besides its olive-green coloration, you can tell it from a white by counting the bucklers (bony plates) in the lateral (side) row. The green has 30 or less; the white always has more.

Because of its qualities as a sport fish, there is a minor fishery for the green. It may even be possible to find a few charter operations specializing part-time in the fish. At a maximum size of seven feet and weight of 350 pounds, it is a fine battler on a stout salmon outfit.

But, happily for the green, it has a bad table reputation. In fact, it is considered by most to be the *only* member of the sturgeon clan that is downright inedible. (Tony's Fish Markets in the Portland area is just one of many companies that disprove that. The source of fish for their excellent smoked sturgeon is Willapa Bay. There's a green commercial fishery in that Washington coastal estuary.) With some local exceptions and prejudices, the basic approaches that work for whites will work for greens.

WHITE STURGEON *(ACIPENSER TRANSMONTANUS)*

"Transmontanus" is a combination of two words handed down from Latin: "trans" means "beyond;" "montanus" means "mountain." Along with its nearly extinct cousin, the Atlantic sturgeon, this magnificent creature is North America's largest freshwater fish.

You will hear it locally called the Pacific sturgeon, the Oregon sturgeon, the Columbia River sturgeon, the Sacramento sturgeon and The Biggest Damned Fish I Ever Saw. This last is far and away the most scientifically accurate.

The history of the West, particularly the far north corner, reeks with its presence and lore. We have already related one of the Snake River legends. A variation of that one tells of a prospector who stopped to try for his dinner at the confluence of the Imnaha and Snake rivers. Feeling the call of nature, he tied his fishing rope (not line, but "rope") to his donkey. You know what he didn't find when he came back, and what had pulled it out into the middle of where.

At the turn of the century, according to news reports, it was common to heave out a meat hook baited with small pieces of big animals or several generations of smaller animals, then tie the line – a clothesline – to a tree and see what happened.

In point of fact, most early, post-pioneer Westerners thought the delectable white a trash fish. It got in their way when they were trying to catch salmon. They killed and discarded it whenever they could. Then markets began to appear. Among others, the San Francisco elite crowd took to it. So, their restaurants did, too. In the manner of all standard human approaches where profit is involved, they got down to the business of catching every sturgeon in

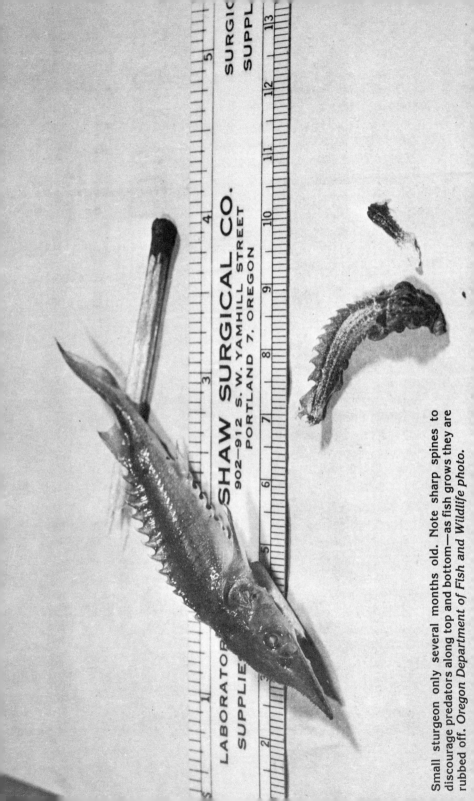

Small sturgeon only several months old. Note sharp spines to discourage predators along top and bottom—as fish grows they are rubbed off. *Oregon Department of Fish and Wildlife photo.*

Sturgeon Fishing

California. When the pickings there got slim, they turned their hungry eyes northward.

Intensive white sturgeon fishing began in Oregon and Washington in 1888. By 1892, the catch was up to 2500 metric tons and valued at $66,000. (That was when $300 would buy a nice house!) Ignorant of the biology of the species, they slaughtered the white in vast numbers via Chinese gang lines, fish traps, fish wheels and seines, bringing it to its fishy knees by the turn of the century.

How can this history be of any use to you? It gives you an excellent reason to meticulously obey present-day sturgeon regulations. Research has shown that this naturally long-lived and slow-growing fish does not come into a reproductive state until it has lived long enough (seven to ten years) to reach a length of roughly three feet. And, that as it reaches lengths beyond six feet, it becomes a sturgeon factory, producing geometrically more eggs.

Taking into account the simple reasoning that one needs some small fish if one is going to have big fish to catch later on, the current regs on most of the West Coast allow the taking of fish *inside* a certain size range. Usually, a check of local laws will indicate that takeable sturgeon must be longer than 36 to 40 inches and shorter than six feet.

(Exception: California, for some ignorant reason, allows the taking of the big females. Their premise is that they prohibit the taking of under 40-inch fish, thus giving every female sturgeon the chance to reproduce at least *once*. Things will get worse there, until someone wakes up. We owe great respect to those California anglers who, through enlightened self-interest and more intelligence than their state officials, observe the six-foot maximum kill.)

If we all respect the regulations, the fishery, which may be slowly but steadily coming back from near disaster and long closures, will just get better and better.

From Monterey to Alaska, we will have the white we almost lost: the world's most magnificent freshwater fish!

Getting to Know the Great White

Chapter 3

Now that you've had a proper introduction to the topic in general, the real work begins. Scratch a sturgeon angler and you'll find one layer of amateur scientist, one layer of natural observer, one layer of bullheaded determination and three layers of the patience of Job.

You can go out on your first trip and catch trout. You can fly to Alaska and down a Dall sheep and be back in camp for tea. But, unless you are as lucky as Gladstone Gander or have a good guide, you won't nail a decent sturgeon on your first – or necessarily your fifth – trip.

In the Pacific Northwest, there is a legend concerning steelhead, the sea-going rainbow trout. It is said they don't exist. This is because some people fish for them for ten years before landing their *first one!* And this fish is *heavily* propagated via government hatchery programs.

There are almost no stocking programs for the sturgeon, outside the Soviet Union and California. (Caviar – sturgeon roe – is an important export for the Soviet Union, and their stocks have been sagging of late due in part to their failure to protect habitat.)

You catch good-sized sturgeon for one of two reasons.

Sturgeon Fishing

One, you are fishing with somebody who knows how, where and when to catch good-sized sturgeon. Two, you devote the time to learning how, where and when to catch good-sized sturgeon.

Just one example will illustrate this truth. Local variations aside (and there are so many of them that we're already in trouble), you catch sturgeon in San Francisco Bay and environs in winter. From October on. You can fish for Columbia whites all year, though most people prefer late winter, spring and summer, particularly the spring.

If you fish too early in the spring, in some locations, you won't do well. In others you can be too late in the spring. To catch the concentrations of sturgeon, you time your activity to the food sources, many of which surge east each year on their spawning runs. But, while you certainly can fish *when* the smelt (for example) are running, things can sometimes be hottest just *after* the runs have peaked. Certainly, there's no harm in working the tailings.

Do the sturgeon smell a big run of baitfish coming upstream and just swim along with them? Do they wait for a run to pass and then tag right behind, picking up the weaker stragglers and wounded ones that come drifting back with the current?

No research we're aware of provides that information. It would be interesting to compare sturgeon catch ratios just before, during and just after a good run of smelt somewhere. (If you decide to do it, base your figures on hours spent divided by the number of fish taken, not just on fish caught. Keep an eye on the sizes, too. Lots of studies indicate that fish of a given size range seem to spend quite a bit of time in the same neighborhood.)

As with the Columbia system, *when* you fish a particular bait in San Francisco Bay can be critically important. There are general rules, such as the time of the herring spawn, which can be limited to a matter of days off certain limited beach areas. But, these change with water conditions to such an extent that on any given day the best bait might be one of *three* different kinds of shrimp: ghost, mud or grass.

Anybody who thinks dry fly fishing for trout is the only angling art is nuts.

So, let's begin the serious work with an in-depth look at the quarry. By understanding what he is, we may understand when and why he does what he does. In the sturgeon business, that kind of knowledge separates the keepers from the shakers.

As we've already said, the sturgeon is of an ancient order. Its ancestors developed prior to the introduction of vertebrates on earth. (Vertebrates, if you've forgotten your high school biology, are animals with an internal support structure of bones. Ribs, a back bone, etc.)

The earliest life on earth was single-celled stuff. Plants, and later, animals. The continental drift theory indicates there was at one time just one big continent and the rest was all ocean. Geological things move more slowly than a highway road repair crew, so there was, as Carl Sagan would put it, BILLIONS and BILLIONS of years for all these planktonic ("plankton" comes from the Greek—it means "drifter") plants and animals to flourish and breed and be born and die in uncounted numbers.

As they perished, they sank to the bottom. It was good fertilizer. In the vast shallow seas that existed during the various ages, where the depths were not too great for a good daily bath of sunlight to come filtering down, entire ecological webs formed. Our friend, the sturgeon, came along to muck about in the goop down there, quietly thundering along with the tides and currents, looking for mollusks (clams and snails), the spawn of other creatures (don't forget, caviar is spawn), reasonably fresh, if a bit mangled, small fish, and the tasty exoskeleton invertebrates that cost ten dollars a pound at least in the supermarket today: shrimp.

Is there any wonder that sturgeon—smoked, baked or just about any other way—tastes so good? Look at what the rascals eat! (In the Columbia system they dine on lamprey eels, too, which puts some delicate western sensibilities off. The French, and most Orientals, feel differently. The

Sturgeon Fishing

author takes no side at all.)

The earliest sturgeon varieties were probably a lot larger than the fish today. Their first aquatic enemies were fearsome monsters that could swallow a metal-hulled charter boat in one gulp and pick their teeth with the stainless steel mast. That's probably why the sturgeon decided to put on armor. Their armor protected them from the nasties until the nasties died out, and old man ocean just kept the food rolling along. As the pieces of the earth drifted to where they are today, the sturgeon just hung out on the local corner and whistled at the passing mollusks.

That explains the slight variations in the fish one finds across and about the globe. Australia has wombats, duck-billed platypuses and kangaroos because the earliest common mammalian stocks were isolated and formed their

In the dark water of the Columbia River 70 feet and more deep the sturgeon quietly searches for food while using its barbels to sense what is good and what is not. *O.H.S. photo no. 78741.*

own local unions with their own local way of looking and doing.

Sturgeon, basically well designed to start with, just made some minor regional adaptations, becoming green or white, big or small. But, wherever they remained, they remained essentially shallow water fish, foraging in the productive "nursery areas" of the continental shelves and into the rivers and bays.

And, that is where you'll find them to this day.

Having fished the Pacific off the Northwest coast for thirty years both as a sports angler and as a deckhand on charter boats, I have never seen a sturgeon caught on hook and line in the open ocean. This is not to say it couldn't be done. For years, the superb Oregon striped bass fishery was contained totally within a few bays and rivers in the vicinity of Coos Bay.

I had a custom twelve-foot, single-piece surf casting rod built, and tried East Coast squidding tactics in an experiment to duplicate the Montauk experience for stripers. I finally gave up, convinced it couldn't be done that way here. Someone else came along and did it after me.

Certainly, there is direct evidence that sturgeon, like stripers, travel the open ocean. And, there is a documented case of a crab fisherman who found a dead forty-incher in a crab pot off the mouth of the Columbia River. but, as I've said, that's not the place to fish for them. Your focus will be the bays and river systems.

Some sturgeon will apparently visit many different river systems during their long lifetimes. Whether they will *spawn* in more than one system, however, is in question.

It was thought for years that steelhead would only spawn in the river of their origin. But, now we know that's not true. When Mount St. Helens blew her top, and her rivers became silted and impassable, some fish turned up in new streams. That event, incidentally, had a dramatic effect on Columbia sturgeon. A large number left the river, particularly on the Washington side, and headed into other river systems.

Sturgeon Fishing

Even without that kind of dramatic incentive, salmon occasionally do the same, it appears. Perhaps it's a natural, if rare, occurrence. If so, it would explain how the range of a species is expanded throughout all available habitable water.

And, that would point toward the sturgeon's existence in virtually every good-sized river system in the West, from tidewater up to the first shallow water or dam without navigation locks or fish ladders. (The biggest sturgeon surely must need navigation locks, rather than ladders, on their upstream runs. Which begs a question. If twenty to forty percent of *downstream* salmonids die in the turbines and nitrogen supersaturation of each dam's flues, how many ten-foot sturgeon have we turned into hamburger while frying our hamburger on our suburban electric ranges?)

Studies in the vicinity of Bonneville Dam on the Columbia have shown that tagged fish move quite a bit – sometimes on the average of close to a mile a day. The same studies, which proved that fish tagged just below the dam were caught later at the mouth, didn't come up with a single return above the dam. Sturgeon are rarely spotted by the fish counters at the ladders, so it's safe to assume that not many of them use the devices.

Sturgeon vary their feeding patterns from area to area. In San Francisco Bay, Abe Cuanang and his pals work the water in winter. Food availability, including herring spawning runs, seems to be the principal dictating factor. The Columbia River Sturgeon Navy as we've already noted goes into action in late winter, spring and summer. Here, the key is the spring smelt run – the eulachon ("you-la-con") migration – anchovie and herring movements or, in summer, the concentrations of lamprey eels.

Note: There are apparently fish who tend to be resident in a small area, and others (probably the majority) who wander around in strung out groups quite a bit.

It would be easy to assume each of these concentrations of sturgeon have geared their reproductive migrations to

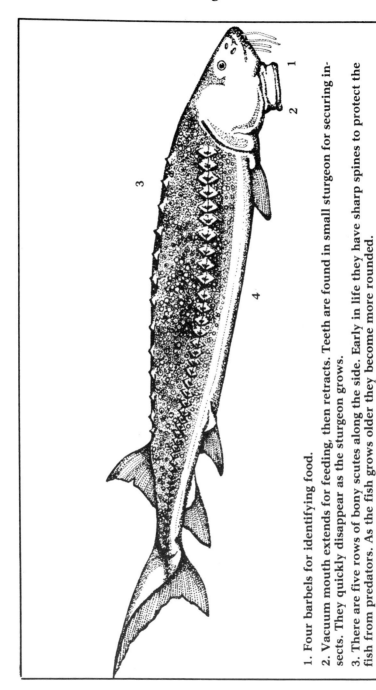

1. Four barbels for identifying food.

2. Vacuum mouth extends for feeding, then retracts. Teeth are found in small sturgeon for securing insects. They quickly disappear as the sturgeon grows.

3. There are five rows of bony scutes along the side. Early in life they have sharp spines to protect the fish from predators. As the fish grows older they become more rounded.

4. Sturgeon are born with a pointed nose which broadens and flattens as the fish grows.

Sturgeon Fishing

the timing of the local baitfish spawning runs. That, in fact, may actually be the case. But, there has been so little actual research done on the big fish, that we're not sure exactly *where* they prefer to spawn, let alone when. Until quite recently, no one had ever seen a juvenile sturgeon.

Studies in California have shown that water temperature may be the true determining factor. When the water warms to something approaching 17°C., that's about right. (To convert Centigrade to Fahrenheit, a good rough scale is to double the C. figure and add 32.)

In any event, anglers have, over the years, discovered by trial and error most of what the biologists now know: When, where and how each area produces the best sturgeon fishing.

Those four barbels just under the nose are like antennae. With them, the fish feels along the bottom. When the sturgeon strikes something that might be food, a reflex action takes place and the suction mouth shoots out to pick it up.

As you can see, a sturgeon has nostrils. They will follow scent trails in the water the way a dog will follow them in the air. It may be that this sense is most useful in a general way—in the location of larger concentrations of food. At any rate, many anglers believe in taking advantage of it, and anoint their baits with all sorts of concoctions. Fish oils of various types, gear oil, WD-40—all have been used at one time or another.

While sturgeon may be found in what seem to be holding areas, they muzzle around within such areas quite a bit, surveying the bottom for what might have recently drifted down. It is likely that creating a scent trail for them will focus their movement in your direction.

Avoid, however, the temptation to just sit back and wait. If you're banking it, you don't have much choice. But, if you're in a boat, it really does pay to test a spot, then move on.

Sooner or later, you'll hit pay dirt.

Tools of the Trade

Chapter 4

Most experts recommend a boat rod in the neighborhood of six and a half to seven feet in length, although I have seen some custom built sticks that were shorter than that. Some of the anglers who work Washington's Chehalis River favor standard salmon mooching rods and reels. They use light line, as well, running down to 20-lb.-test on the theory that any fish they can't land with that they'd have to throw back, anyway.

A standard sturgeon model by LCI that I saw at Larry's Sporting Goods in Cedar Hills, Oregon, was very close to five feet in length. It had good quality roller guides and sold for about a hundred and forty dollars.

It is perhaps arguable that a shorter rod offers a better balance when fighting a big fish in the sense that it is easier to hold a shorter stick than a longer one. The battle point of balance, the fighting fulcrum, would be closer to the angler.

Most guides, however, go for something in the six to seven foot range.

Whatever you go with, it should be one piece and have a strong lower section and a "fast" tip. The reasons for these requirements are simple, and have behind them years of

Sturgeon Fishing

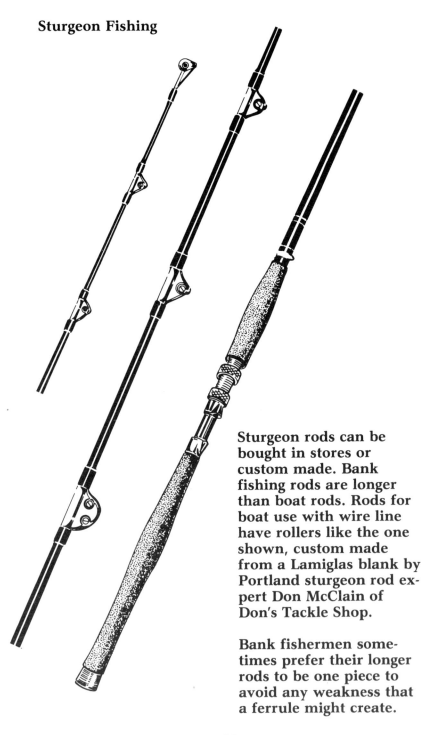

Sturgeon rods can be bought in stores or custom made. Bank fishing rods are longer than boat rods. Rods for boat use with wire line have rollers like the one shown, custom made from a Lamiglas blank by Portland sturgeon rod expert Don McClain of Don's Tackle Shop.

Bank fishermen sometimes prefer their longer rods to be one piece to avoid any weakness that a ferrule might create.

experimentation.

The short salmon boat rods are meant for smaller fish. A big chinook might run forty pounds. A forty-pound sturgeon is not a very big fish, at all. When you're fighting a fish that outweighs *you,* you may need a little beef. The bigger stick gives you that. (At the price of a little less freedom for the fish to let 'er rip.)

The strong butt is a necessity for a similar reason. A lot of torque transfers down the rod when you're hooked to seven feet of fish. If the rod isn't able to take it, you'll be left standing there with some splinters in your hand.

Although sometimes big sturgeon will simply pick up bait and take off with it, as a rule they will tug gently. The sucker mouth and barbels were designed to sift through the detritus on the bottom and quickly identify it as food or something else. The feeding pattern of a sturgeon, for all its tremendous size, is *delicate.* It is often impossible to tell whether those gentle taps are a ten inch bullhead or a ten foot white. (For the novice, anyway.)

A sensitive tip is therefore important.

(NOTE: I hate to do this to you, because it'll leave some confusion in your mind, BUT, don't get an *overly* sensitive tip, either. There's a reason why the area around Cascade Locks in Oregon has become the windsurfing capital of the world. Big water means big wind. That means chop. A too sensitive tip would look like a yo yo under those conditions.)

Why should it be one piece? Because every time you put a joint in a rod (just like every time you tie a knot in a line), *that* becomes a weak spot.

If you're using monofilament line, any quality guide system will do. Bear in mind that the "fatter" the guide surface, the less likely you are to have cutting or wearing, especially under the stress of a big fish. Casting is not a factor, here, so the increased drag of a greater surface area is not a problem. Many experts recommend aluminum oxide as a guide insert surface, as you don't have the grooving problems you do with just chrome.

Sturgeon Fishing

Penn, long famous for its big star drag reels, just recently came out with a line of matching rods. Some of these look interesting for our purposes. Their International II rods, models I.G.F.A. 30W (30-50 lb. line) and I.G.F.A. 50W (50-80 lb. line), are the right length, seven feet. They've got a roller guide system that should handle wire just fine. A price list wasn't available at press time, but they're made of top grade stuff. They'll be spendy.

Probably more moderate in cost is their International series. Models IGFA 30WSU, 30W and 50W are possibilities. Another step down, we find the Senator series of rods. The 3/0 S2-3030ARA and 6/0 S2-3060ARA offer roller guides from top to bottom. (I'm not sure I like those metal butts, though.) The other models have bottom and top roller guides with eyelet style guides in between.

Wire line requires roller guides.

The best roller guide rods have a *double* guide at the bottom. This helps the line feed evenly on and off the spool. That's important with wire, as that material, even though braided for flexibility, can twist and kink on you.

Leaving wire line models for the moment, some other rods you might consider are Penn's Power Stick (PC-3721MH), and one of their Slammer series: the SLC-2701AX. It is seven feet long, handles 20-50 lb. line and up to six ounces of weight, which would be fine for most of the lighter current situations. As a bonus, this rod has double-braced chrome-plated stainless steel aluminum oxide guides and tip.

One advantage of selecting tackle from a company that offers both rods and reels is that you can easily match the two of them. The manufacturer has tested the gear in advance and can recommend a specific range of reels from which you can choose and still have a balanced outfit.

I've always enjoyed using Fenwick equipment. Take a look at their I.G.F.A. 30 and 50 models, and, from their Pacificstik line, models PR1665HC (30-80 lb. line, up to 8 oz. of weight) and PR1670C, which is longer, but lighter in build.

Abe Cuanang, in his superb *San Francisco Bay Sturgeon* (see "Acknowledgements") says he likes Fenwick's Pacificstiks and Pacificstik Royales. The models he prefers are the 789-C, rated for 15-50 (mono) line and the 1870-C, rated for 15 to 40 lb. stuff.

Abe Cuanang may be the world's greatest sturgeon angler, so if you don't plan on working the super heavy water that requires wire line, don't hesitate to take *his* advice.

And, now that it's come up, there's a problem we haven't really faced up to here. In truth, some Northwest sturgeon fishing situations require more than eight ounces of weight. Sometimes, guide Gary Krum sends up to forty eight ounces down into the early spring turbulence below the Columbia's Bonneville Dam. That explains why he, like many other sturgeon fans, has has rods custom built. If you're going to have to deal with conditions like this, you're going to have to locate a local tackle shop that understands what you need.

Rod materials are your choice, though some of the new compounds offer great strength for less weight. Should you have to hang onto that rod for four hours, a couple of ounces might make your afternoon slightly easier.

BANK OUTFITS

Most bankers prefer much longer rods. Lamiglas, a company in Woodland, Washington, builds a model known as the SB11 HC. It's eleven feet long and of good quality. I've seen it packaged in sporting goods stores as a combo, teamed with the Daiwa 350H reel. The price was a little over two hundred dollars.

Another Lamiglas model, the SB 10 MHC, is a good one, too. If you were going to stick with the Daiwa reel, you could use the 50H. This reel, incidentally, is one of the most popular for this kind of angling. A lot of trolling and casting reels have two piece spools. Monofilament line will load up during a long fight, spreading the side plates. A one piece spool prevents separation of the side plates. You can get a combo like this for something in the neighborhood of a hundred and fifty bucks.

Fenwick offers a series they call Atlanticstiks. Two of them, the ASU1445 (12-ft., 3 to 6 oz. lure weight capability, 15-30 lb. line) and the ASU1328-2 (11-ft., 4 to 6 oz. lure weight, 20-50 lb. line) look interesting. These rods were designed for long surf casts, and would be worth an inspection to see if they might be good for our purposes.

The sensitive tip of the boat rod is not necessarily a benefit here, because of the way bank fishing has evolved.

If you read the first chapter of this book, you noticed that the bite was like what we describe in boat angling situations. The sliding sinker setup is still utilized by bank anglers today, and thus a relatively quick tip is right. Willamette River anglers in the vicinity of Oregon City will work the bite that way, and you will see that method used elsewhere, too.

But, a number of banking variations have come along over the years. Until it was deemed illegal, some bankers utilized various types of self-powered "model" boats, or rafts, that they would send out to the water they wanted to fish. Then, they would pull the sinker off and let it sink. The "boat" was connected to a line that was then retrieved.

As has been mentioned, that method is no longer legal anywhere we know of in the Northwest.

These days you will see yet another technique in use.

A long, beefy rod is used to pick up a heavy weight on a light testing dropper and heave it a long ways. Once the weight is set on the bottom, the reel can be cranked under a locked down drag until a strong rod bow is formed. When the sturgeon takes the bait, and either breaks the lead line or tugs the weight free, the rod has the power and sweep to set the hook at least in a preliminary fashion.

Bankers use standard, levelwind and spinning gear. In all cases, we're talking about monofilament line. Since heavy monofilament creates a lot of drag, it is wise to have a good set of guides.

The cheaper rods will have poor quality guides, in general. In the case of spinning rods they will be too small and have improper spacing and diameters one to the other.

There are many kinds of "ceramic" guides on the market. Get aluminum oxide inserts if you can.

The secret to a smooth casting spinning rod, besides having the spool properly filled, is an evenly spaced "cone" of guides of descending diameter. Bear in mind that there is a kind of balance between the guides and a rod blank. Just as you can have too few guides (the most common situation with cheaper, softer action rods) it is possible to have too many guides for a given blank. The resulting product would be much stiffer than you might want. That stiffness could rob you of wind-up torque, thus distance.

No matter which type of angling you plan on doing, make sure the rod is the best you can afford. Talk to a custom rodmaker. See what he might recommend. Go to your local sporting goods stores. Take a look at the kind of gear they have to offer.

But, if you can't afford it right now, go ahead and give the old mooching outfit a try. If it came to that, you ought to be able to catch a buster sturgeon on a standard *steelhead outfit*. Take some extra line if you try it, though. These fish have stripped one or two reels to the spool.

REELS

Bankers using spinning gear will want something originally designed for saltwater use. Make sure the bail system is the best you can find. You don't need a malfunction in that area in the middle of a fight. And, take a long, hard look at the drag system. It has to be 1) both rugged and smooth in operation, and 2) accessible.

The reason for the first is obvious. So should the reason for the second. There is no time to fumble awkwardly for the drag adjustment when you have a freight train on the line. It must be easily reached and simple to operate.

Don't test it by pulling out line while standing in the

store. Put the reel on a rod. Have a friend grab the line and start running down an aisle. If you can adjust it smoothly under those conditions, it's a good one.

The Cadillac. The Penn 50TW is a low profile, wide-framed reel. It will handle 600 yards of 80-lb. mono line. You don't often need this much reel, of course, but it sure is a classy looking job. (Wire-line reels generally have much narrower spools.) *Photo courtesy of Penn Reels.*

The best reel for a boat setup is the standard (or, for some anglers, the levelwind). A good star drag from a quality company will do just fine. If it is to hold mono, you'l need a 350 yd. capacity of the line weight you decide to use. That means a 3/0 or 4/0 size, usually.

Make sure that the drag system is extremely smooth, rugged and handy to operate. You'll be setting the hook with a tight drag and then immediately backing it off.

America's most famous maker of reels is, of course, Penn. Their 3/0 Senator runs about sixty-five dollars, and has landed its share of sturgeon hereabouts. It's their model 112. The 113 is bigger, 4/0, and is popular, too.

(Those of you who drive Cadillacs could get the Penn International 20. You can pack on a quarter mile of 40 lb. test mono on one of these wide-framed, gold anodized aluminum, chrome-plated brass hummers. Because of that wide-frame design, these units let you wind on heavier stuff easily, too. All you do is lose some yardage. In the case of this reel, there's so much room it won't make a whit of difference. If this one is too big for your outfit, take a look at the 12T.)

If you're a levelwinder, their 209MS (larger rod stand) or 209MF (smaller rod stand) have decent line capacity at the lower end of line tests.

ABU Garcia makes a monster called the XLVI with a 4.5:1 gear ratio that holds 400 yds. of 30 lb. test line. (Or 300 yds. of 40 lb.). Their XLV holds 500 yds. of 20 lb. and 300 yds. of 30 lb. Both of these are levelwinders, too.

Daiwa makes some popular standards. At one local store I found their 50H at $55, their 300H for $70 and their 350H priced at $75. The 50H is a standard for both boat and bank anglers.

Shimano has an interesting line of reels they call Triton. Their TLD 10 will hold 300 yds. of 20 lb. mono. The TLD 15 will hold 350 yds. of 25 lb. line. They have a lever drag system with some fascinating features. Unlike a standard star drag, there's only one thing to grab. The way they've got it set up, you can select a given drag situation and then by manipulation of the drag lever over a short arc, increase or decrease the drag almost instantly. Finally, when you want to return to the original setting, you can do that instantly. The 4.2:1 gear ratio on these reels is just about right.

When you're boat fishing, you want a locked down drag for the strike and then the fastest possible way to release to a fighting drag. This reel is designed for just that kind of action.

Shimano also makes a Triton star drag series. The gear

ratio is 5:1. That's a bit hotter than some sturgeon reels. Could be handy when you're trying to keep a weight off the bottom or reel in, or when a fish is charging directly at you. The line capacity on their TSD 4S is good.

If you're interested in getting a reel that might do a little double duty, take a look at Shimano's Triton levelwind moden TRN 200GT or the larger TRN 300. The mono capacity of either of these reels is adequate. Some anglers prefer the levelwind, anyway.

If you're going to be using wire line, make sure the reel's surfaces are capable of handling it cleanly, and without excessive wear.

Wire line reels have a special characteristic that sets them apart. They all have much narrower spools. As has been noted elsewhere, this limits the loading travel span. It saves trouble.

Penn makes a line of these specialty reels. It's called their narrow spool Mariner series. Depending on the weight of the outfit you're trying to match, you might want their 49L, 149L or 349H model. Likely, it'll be one of the first two.

LINE

The only thing connecting you and the fish hook is your line. Never use line that because of exposure (to sunlight, for example, in the case of mono) may have deteriorated. If there is any question, replace it.

Some anglers like Andy line. It's inexpensive, and resists abrasion well.

I use Maxima mono for everything from ultralight trout fishing to sturgeon. It is supple (relatively limp) and takes a knot without excessive test loss. Some people think I'm nuts. You may prefer some other manufacturer. What's important is that the stuff you use doesn't stretch any more than absolutely necessary, and doesn't cut easily.

Inspect it regularly for abrasions. When you're fighting a big bruiser, your line can saw across a lot of different

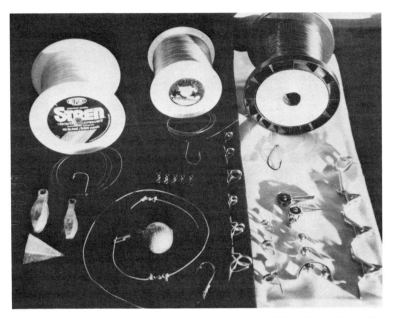

Note the ball-sinker rocky bottom rigging. A slider like this, with varying amounts of free play, gets the bait where the fish are. The fish won't feel any resistance when he takes the bait, and he doesn't have to drag the sinker to let your tip know you have something going on down there. *Photo by Christopher Fesler.*

things out there. It's a shame not to even see the biggest fish you'll probably ever hook just because your line was bad.

If you're picking up a new reel anyway, have them wind the line on with one of those fixed tension devices. That will guarantee that at least once you don't have the possibility of uneven tension loops forming. You may hook a ten footer on your first cast!

(Don't laugh. That happened on the Columbia one recent day. I saw it. When that fish came out of the water not ten feet from the boat it looked like a submarine launched missile exploding into the sky. Ten foot long fish tail-walking less than their own length from you are impressive sights, indeed. You seriously consider walking home.)

What test should it be? In places like the Fraser River,

the Columbia/Snake system or San Francisco Bay, your odds of hooking something quite large are quite good. Abe Cuanang suggests fifty pound test for beginners, though he himself favors thirty to forty pound stuff. (If you're going to use these tests, make sure your reel will hold *at least* 275 yards of it.)

Wire line cuts through heavy water better than mono. A thousand feet of it will run you about thirty bucks. *Photo by Christopher Fesler.*

But, in some of the smaller systems, you can do quite well with twenty- or twenty-five pound test. If the rare big one grabs, you'll just have to set the drag light and plan on spending the weekend in the boat.

Sturgeon live in places with little light. Their eyes are tiny and of little use to them. Often, the best time to fish for them is when the water is a bit off color. As far as I can tell, you could use a dayglo red line and it wouldn't make a whit of difference, so decide for yourself what you want in that department.

Wire line is the route many sturgeon anglers take under heavy current situations. When you're dealing with the heavy spring flows below the Columbia's Bonneville Dam, mono presents all sorts of unnecessary difficulties.

Weights required to hold a bait down may run as high as 48 ounces! Mono has a lot of drag, and thus tends to try to raise the weight from the bottom. By the time you add enough weight to keep the mono down, you need a winch to drag it back up.

Wire cuts more cleanly through the water, has weight of its own and is certainly strong enough to handle any fish.

Sevenstrand wire is available in most good sporting goods outlets. A thousand feet of it runs up near thirty bucks. Weller makes a line they call Seacraft. It sells for about the same price.

WEIGHTS

It's an axiom of sturgeon angling that these fish, being muckrakers, are not fond of rocky bottoms. Knowing the feeding habits makes that clear. Yet, many places where sturgeon are found – perhaps just traveling through – one finds rocks.

Bankers will tie on some railroad tie spikes, a big rock or anything else they don't mind losing. When you expect the lead line to snap, you don't want to invest a fortune in special lead. The problem with these, however, is that they are akward to cast and tend to get snagged. If you get tired of fooling with them, try ball lead. It'll cost more when you lose one, but you won't lose as many.

Boat fishing is different.

You'll be working in a current. It'll be a tidal flow or the sweeping waters of a river. In general, you'll want to walk the bait downstream a ways from where you are anchored. It isn't that there are more sturgeon the farther you get from the boat, but rather that the line will lay out a little flatter.

This accomplishes three things.

One: it decreases friction, or drag, that the fish can feel at the slip sinker junction. (If the line goes straight down, it has to turn a sharp corner to go through the slider – or loop, or swivel – whichever you use). The drag could alert a fish that what he is mouthing is not what it appears to be.

Two: a flatter line to bait angle means a truer reading of the bite. The sharp downward angle could actually force the fish to lift the sinker in the process. (Put a heavy washer on a foot long string. Run it down toward one end. Lift the short end. Yup, the washer will lift.) And, even if that doesn't happen, the extra drag will disguise the true nature of the bite.

Three: when you set the hook, a flatter line means less of a pickup angle – less slack – that has to be taken up by the rod's arc before you're sinking that hook.

Since the best depth finder can't give you an exact reading of every little rock and snag down there, use lead ball weights. Being round, they will have less tendency to get snagged on anything. (Or stuck in anything.)

Lead ball weights have eyes sticking out of them, which is handy. You can put a snap at the bottom of your sliding lead line and quickly change to match conditions.

HOOKS

A 6/0 Siwash is the most popular sturgeon hook around. Sometimes it's used alone, sometimes in tandem with a mooching slider. Old Van Elliot favored a big treble on the end of leader threaded through a baitfish.

THE STURGEON BOAT

Guide Gary Krum uses the boat shown here. It's a big jet sled. Since he guides in all sorts of fresh and saltwater situations, it's a compromise of sorts. What it has going for it is a strong power train.

Generally, most sturgeon addicts go with something else.

If you're going to fish big water, make sure you've got the freeboard and power to deal with big water. When current flow demands wire line and 48 ounces of lead, when wind chop comes suddenly your way, when a squall races across the water and slams into you like a hammer . . . you need enough boat to keep fishing, or, in some cases, alive.

When you fish from a boat, you are anchored. If you're downstream from a dam, flow can change. Without a goodly amount of power, you can be left hanging on the end of an anchor line unable to drive upcurrent to retrieve it.

That, incidentally, is one reason why experienced sturgeon boat anglers utilize an anchor line buoy. Anchors, particularly the rigs handiest in big water, do not come cheap. If you have to lose the line, hopefully to chase a big sturgeon, the buoy allows relocation.

Certain barrel buoys now in use are designed to slide down the line when you're ready to pull up stakes. They float the anchor up from the bottom for you. Absolutely gold, one of those!

Anyway, returning to the point of all this, if your boat is

The adventure begins. Famous Northwest guide Gary Krum and legendary angler Lee Tomerlin prepare to leave a Columbia River beach near Cascade Locks. *Photo by Larry Leonard.*

not strong enough for the Columbia in flood, concentrate on smaller river/bay systems until things calm down.

Finally, look favorably on a craft that is rock stable. You'll be standing when you're fighting a fish. The waters where sturgeon live are not nice places to fall in.

SPECIAL AIDS

After the tackle, and if you can afford it, perhaps the single most important item of fishing gear you can have on board is a good depth finder. In the smaller rivers, it's not as important, but in the bays and larger rivers, a depth finder is invaluable.

Here's how Abe Cuanang sees it, writing in his superb *San Francisco Bay Sturgeon:*

"The use of electronics has been employed and adapted in many fields, especially so in the sport of fishing. Depth locators or graphs which specifically employ the use of bouncing sonar waves off solid objects can give an angler a precise depth of the bottom, point out its subtle irregularities, and accurately determine the level fish are holding at."

Cuanang goes on to point out a basic of bay sturgeon behavior that you will find is discussed all through this manual; namely, that if you're going to find any sort of concentration of them moving or feeding it'll be along ledges or slopes. (Except in the dead of winter in the Columbia, when you will often find them slugged down in the pits of the deepest holes, this rule holds true in the big bays, too.)

Put simply, if you're in an unknown area, or one that might have reconfigured its bottom via winter storms or floods, there is no greater asset than a depth finder.

What kind?

Lowrance is a good name. Cuanang swears by the X-15.

Humminbird has a fine line. Their LCR 4000 covers (graphically and digitally) depths of 120 feet in four "zero to" ranges with zoom capability. They've done some development work to add to shallow water performance.

Their liquid crystal displays are good sized, sharp, and computer controlled to de-emphasize surface clutter. Less expensive, and thus with fewer bells and whistles, are the LCR 2000 and 1000.

The bottom of things. There have been some amazing advances in depth sounder technology in recent years. A machine like this can turn a skunking into a banner day. Sturgeon are definitely *where* you find them. Shown: Humminbird's LCR 3004. *Photo courtesy of Humminbird U.S.A.*

How to Find the Sturgeon

Chapter 5

With few exceptions, most sturgeon will be found in one of three major West Coast locations: San Francisco Bay and related waters, the Columbia system, and the Fraser. The reason? Simple. A sturgeon does not reach peak reproductive age until it's been alive long enough to grow to a length of six feet or more.

It takes a lot of food to fill the belly of a fish that size. A big river comes with a lot of food. Secondly, a big fish is probably more comfortable in a big river.

Thus, if a big fish likes a particular system, that's where the little fish will be born.

The biologists might give some other reasons, like spawning habitat of sufficient quality. And, there's probably more to it than that, since there are quite a few rivers that enter the Columbia, but apparently very few of them qualify as spawning grounds.

But, just because you live in Eureka, Coos Bay or Olympia, it doesn't mean you can't find a place to fish. While the concentrations may be smaller, the peak times staggered and of short duration, and the fish smaller—perhaps even transient in nature—there is no harm in taking a stab at it.

46

(Remember somebody figured out how to surf fish for stripers near Coos Bay after I tried and failed.)

Any fairly good sized river, preferably with some sort of a bay at its mouth, from the Golden Gate to Alaska, may harbor the critters. You could be the first to catch them! (Or, more likely, you will discover an underground cadre of anglers who just don't talk about their small fishery to strangers.)

This, incidentally, has been particularly true following the 1980 eruption of Mount St. Helens. The backwash from that titanic event caused some dramatic changes in a number of local rivers – mostly temporary, but a few permanent in nature.

There was a major relocation of sturgeon stocks following the eruption. It has harmed some angling areas, and significantly improved others.

Assuming that you can't locate anybody who knows whether or not the water you're interested in holds sturgeon, use this chapter as your guide.

FIRST: Determine if the place you want to fish has enough water to support a three foot fish. Tillamook County, Oregon's Kilchis River may have some nice chum salmon, steelhead and blueback runs, but two feet of water over sharp boulders is not a likely place to locate a thirty-six inch sturgeon. That is the smallest sturgeon it is legal to keep in most places. (Check your local regs. They do vary. Oregon, for example, now requires a *Sturgeon Tag!*).

SECOND: Determine what the bottom is like. All things being equal, which they never are, sturgeon prefer non-rock bottoms. (For feeding. Spawning may be, and probably is, a different matter.) Understanding this, you will forever wonder why they are so often caught amongst the rocks. Maybe there is sand between the rocks. Who knows?

Sturgeon Fishing

THIRD: Locate a *baitfish* expert who has some information about the place. Believe it or not, there are people who spend a large part of their lives studying those species. The fish and game people in your area can put you on the right track – hopefully. Anyway, if you can't find anybody, talk to the people who supply the bait for other kinds of fishing in the area. They'll know what lives there year-round and what else comes through when.

FOURTH: If you can't even get a handle on that, try to figure it out for yourself. Sturgeon just love mollusks, sucking these creatures right up out of the bottom goo, digesting them and defecating the shells. Guide Gary Krum says that the little shells you find on the Oregon side beaches at Cascade Locks are evidence of exactly that. They'll eat night crawlers, crabs, crawfish, shrimp and just about anything else that comes a tumbling down with the flow.

(In our opinion, the argument that sturgeon offer some sort of threat to salmon and steelhead populations is bunk. Sturgeon don't lurk behind a bush till a school of steelhead smolts comes within range and then surge out like JAWS, vicious teeth agape in a murderous run through the little fish. They have sucker mouths. What they get is either already dead or mortally injured. There is some anecdotal evidence that sturgeon *may* push their way through baitfish packs in tidal areas in order to injure some of them. But, the ultimate argument against this particular bigotry is that during the period of highest Columbia River sturgeon population levels, you could walk from Portland to Vancouver on the backs of the steelhead and salmon. Sturgeon are no significant threat to anadromous species.)

FIFTH: Get the freshest of that kind of bait you can, put it (or them) on a hook, rig a sliding sinker above it and drop it in sturgeon territory.

Note: The basic sliding sinker rig is universal to this kind of angling. It consists of a large swivel tied between the line and up to four feet of leader.

On the upper section, the main line section, you put a

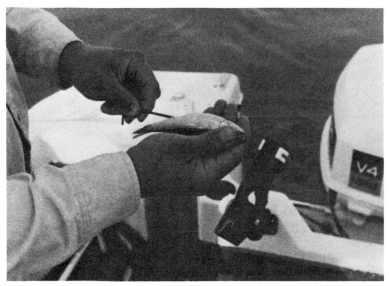

Threading the needle. Sturgeon like to take baitfish head first, so thread the leader through the vent and out the mouth. *Photo by Larry Leonard.*

Hang 'em high. After pulling the hook flush into the mouth, take a few half hitches, working toward the tail. *Photo by Larry Leonard.*

Sturgeon Fishing

The complete rig. Note the sliding sinker in this case is pyramidal. That's the one for holding in soft mud or sand bottom situations. The hook is a lone treble. You can add an upper single if you like. *Photo by Larry Leonard.*

A sturgeon sandwich. A big salmon mooching setup (with a sliding upper hook) is often used for multiple-bait hookups. A chunk of preserved or fresh herring or other baitfish, perhaps a hunk of lamprey eel, a nose-down crayfish and a gob of night crawlers—all can be impaled on the same hook, then thread-wrapped to keep them there. *Photo by Larry Leonard.*

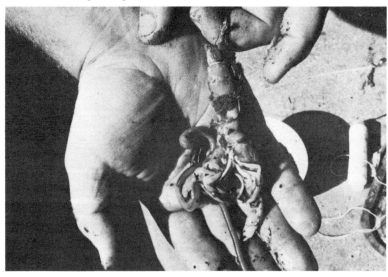

The *piece de resistance!* What French chef worth his salt would present a main course without the proper sauce? (Sturgeon favor WD-40.) *Photo by Larry Leonard.*

"slider." Usually, a tube with a ring where a weight dropper can be attached. (Any tackle shop has them.) Boaters don't need a long weight dropper. If you like, put a snap swivel on the slider ring and clip it directly to the ring on the lead weight. That way you can change weights quickly to find the right one, and adapt to changing conditions faster, too. There's one other advantage to this method. It keeps the bait closer to the bottom.

At the end of the leader, tie a big hook or hooks. A 6/0 is fine.

Some anglers like a double hook salmon mooching rig. Others tie a big treble down there. Others use wire leader and loop the end of the leader, slide on a couple of single hooks back to back and close the loop with a plier-clamped leader sleeve.

SIXTH: Sturgeon territory is usually a channel or a hole. We know people who have caught them cruising like bonefish in the flats of the Columbia mouth at high slack tide, but even these folks spend virtually all of their time in the prime territory. That means a dropoff of some kind that is adjacent to a current.

NOTE: We are not (often) talking about the bottom of the channel or hole. We are talking about the *sides.* Either side of a channel or the *upcurrent* side of a hole. (Thus, the best spot in a hole will change if the current is tidal in nature.)

An exception to this in some areas is during the extreme cold water of mid-winter. You may find them literally holed up, right down there in the deepest part of the deepest hole.

(In the vicinity of Bonneville Dam, experience indicates you should keep an open mind about this advice.)

During low, clear water periods, they hole up. During heavy water periods, you can work closer to shore. The Columbia reacts to the winter rains, of course, but the big water flow comes in late May or June, mostly. Snow runoff is what does it.

So, winter flows are often way down. As the water is also cooler at this time, you can decide for yourself why they hole up.

SEVENTH: Methodically work three or four adjacent spots during each tide/time of day/time of year/etc. set of changing conditions. If the trash fish and crustaceans are robbing you blind, a difference of a few feet in location can make a dramatic difference in the bite. Don't wait longer than a half an hour in one spot unless expert local advice orders the contrary. If you get a fish or a bite or two, and then nothing, move a ways *with* the prevailing current or tide. Particularly in tidal areas, the result may be a fish.

EIGHTH: Keep some sort of mental or written record of what happens.

A FEW TIPS

FINDING FISH: If you don't have any local information, or a chart showing bottom contours, cruise along with an eye on your electronic fish finder. The channels and holes will show on that. And, because of the size of the fish, so will they.

A problem with the latter is that the sturgeon is a bottom hugger. Not all recorders can define a fish hovering a foot or less from the bottom.

If you're lucky, you'll see them jumping in some locations. What is interpreted as a bad sign by river salmon anglers — jumping fish — is often a good sign for sturgeon anglers. (At least you know they're there!)

But remember we said "often." That doesn't mean always. You can be surrounded by an explosion of boxcar-sized fish emerging from the water and be unable to entice a nibble. We haven't come across a good explanation why sturgeon do jump or roll, but they do.

At any rate, fight the tendency to race off at top speed to where a fish has appeared. For all their size, sturgeon are sensitive to their environment. An unusual amount of racket can flush them like a covey of quail.

There's no point in trying to track down singles when you can drop your bait in front of the whole Russian army.

Jumpers may indicate one of those occasional schools of sturgeon holding or passing through an area. They are a clannish fish at times, and have the habit of flocking with similar fish. Just the way a group of monkeys or most herd mammals do, the younger sturgeon will tend to work in one group, the older ones in another.

Whether that holds true when you get up to the truly large fish, say beyond six or seven feet in length, we don't know. After you've angled for them for some time, you'll form your own opinion. For our money, the actual schooling process takes place mostly with smaller fish. With the larger ones, it's more the fact that they happen to be loosely together in a vicinity because feeding patterns and

Sturgeon Fishing

migrating demands push them in that direction.

WATER CONDITIONS favorable for sturgeon angling are determined by the effect those water conditions have on the feeding pattern.

In general, though, the color of water that will send a steelhead angler back to his car brings a smile to the weathered countenance of a sturgeon addict. A little roily with not too much chop is more than okay. The calmer the water, the more easily you can detect the often delicate strike.

TIDES are alternating river currents as far as our quarry is concerned. They move things around one way or another. In an area like Tillamook Bay, they stir up and scour the bottom four times a day. If you had a movie camera that took time lapse photos, and had it take a frame every thirty seconds during an outgoing tide, then ran the film back at normal speed, what happens to the bay would be fascinatingly obvious.

Jerry Luttratt with baby sturgeon he caught and released near Cape Horn on the Columbia.

How to Find the Sturgeon

It isn't just a matter of all the water flowing straight toward the narrow channel between the north and south jetties. At first it's like that, but later another effect takes place. Because there are higher and lower conformations to the bottom topography, and because water likes to hang together like some sort of molecular glue, both gravity and a kind of elastic tension come into play. The water, and thus the tide-carried food, tends to funnel into the channels.

Now, if you were a lazy old sturgeon, interested in socking down the greatest volume of chow for the least effort, where would *you* station yourself?

The channels get the first water on the way in, too.

Another thing you'll notice, particularly in a bay, though it's true in a river under differing flow conditions, is the fact that the border area between what is more or less slack and what is main, strong current, *shifts* in a given area as a tide progresses.

Think of it as a river that widens or narrows before your eyes. In this case, it would be more accurate to call it a river within a lake, since we're talking about what happens in a bay.

At any rate, this shift of the imaginary "banks" of our main current river is important. Keep on top of it, and you will have the best chance of taking fish. Fail to follow its shifting boundaries and you'll either catch nothing or wonder what was working fifteen minutes ago that isn't working now.

As far as the *time* you should fish a given tide, it's pretty generally accepted all up and down the coast that the hours immediately adjacent to either high or low slack are when you should be hitting it hard.

That is, the two hours on either side of a slack.

As we've noted, the varying levels of the bottom topography affect the way the water moves around. For that reason, especially early in your sturgeon exploration period, you should fish the whole tide.

Sturgeon Fishing

If you're really intent on learning how to fish your particular salty stretch of heaven – if you'd like to be one of those sturgeon geniuses like Cuanang or Krum – try the following.

Make a clear plastic grid and place it over a chart of your bay. Number the blocks. Some will have major channels and holes. Others will just show gradually sloping bottoms.

Now, get scientific.

Keep a record of when and what you hook.

It might look something like this:

Date	Tide/Time	Size	Bait	Water	Wt.	Grid
7/4/86	L plus 1	2 ft.	sand shrimp	clear	6	15
8/1/86	L plus 2	4 ft.	worms/shrimp	clear	5	15
10/12/86	H minus 1.5	2 ft.	sand shrimp	clear	5	9
10/14/86	L plus 3	3 ft.	worms/shrimp	clear	5	9
10/23/86	H minus 1	5 ft.	herring	muddy	10	9
10/24/86	H minus 1	5 ft.	herring	muddy	10	9
10/24/86	H minus 2	4 ft.	herring	muddy	12	9

The TIDE/TIME listing calls not for the time of day, but the time of the tide before and after a slack. "Wt." refers to the weight of the lead you were using at the time. It will tell you, among other things, how heavy the water flow was on that day. The other listings should be self-explanatory. Log the time of day, water temperature, weather conditions, surface texture or anything else you like. This is the information age, you know.

Logging the *tide range* could be really informative.

After a few years of doing this, and perhaps sticking a colored pin (with a different color for each season of the year – say green for spring, red for summer, yellow for fall and blue for winter) in each grid location where you take or hook a fish, you're going to be able to do a little analysis.

Some of those grids will be loaded with pins. Others will be empty, even though they look good on the chart and in your recorder screen.

But, if you use just the pins, you'll be missing the best information you can have.

One location may be hot in October when some baitfish migration is in. You'll know that because all the pins are yellow. You may catch half your yearly total there in a single two week period.

But, further analysis may tell you it's always under a specific set of physical conditions. For the sake of argument, we'll say all those yellow pins came over the gunwales when you were using *ten* ounces of weight. Four ounces more than normal for that spot at other times of year. That means either you are fishing just after the fall rains flood the bay, or during tidal ranges that are relatively large. (When the difference between the high and low tides is substantial, which means a lot of water is churning through the area.)

Don't be surprised if that last actually occurs. A big tide range often stimulates decent sturgeon fishing.

But, then, that spot may go dead as a doornail for the other eleven months and two weeks.

Information like that is worth more than an insider stock tip. All you can get with those is rich. All you can get with this is *happy!*

What the rascals do during slack periods is in question, but in some areas it may signal a move to what we could consider non-traditional feeding areas. If you can't bring yourself to go in, and the holes and channel edges are dead, defy common wisdom.

At high slack, some of the fish may drift across flooded flats or along beach areas. Certainly, baitfish can be seen from time to time thrashing about in half-submerged grassy flats. It may be that they find some semblance of protection from predators there, and perhaps a part of their diet in the form of small life forms attaches to the stems.

There is no harm in playing a longshot and methodically working some of these shallower areas. You may happily learn something about sturgeon that nobody else knows!

Another thing you might try is these same areas during prime time – when the tide is running.

In fact, some large expanses of relatively shallow water

Sturgeon Fishing

San Francisco Bay sturgeon rig using wire leader and crimps.

— to line

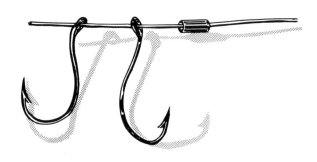

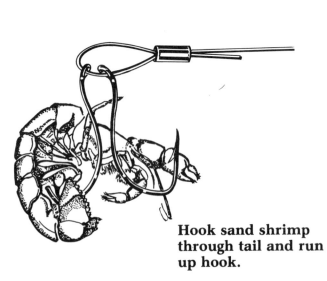

Hook sand shrimp through tail and run up hook.

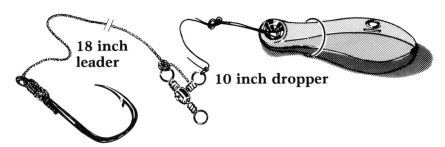

Columbia River sturgeon rig for bank fishing. Weight is looped and tied with smaller strength line for easy break-off. Weight can also be railroad spike, spark plug, etc.

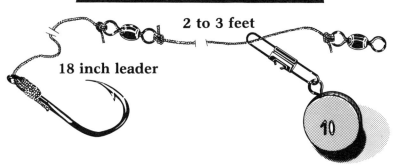

Columbia River sturgeon rig for boat fishing with sliding sinker and clip for easy weight change. Round ball lead.

San Francisco Bay sliding sinker rig
with pyramid sinker.

Sturgeon Fishing

Palomar knot used for tying swivel to main line and leader. Swivel keeps bait from twisting on the bottom and fouling leader.

Snelling sturgeon hook to 100-lb.-test dacron line with bait holder loop.

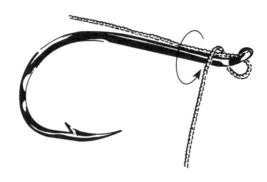

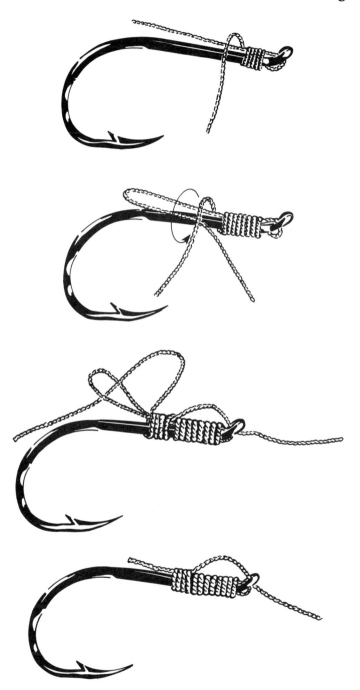

61

consistently produce sturgeon, and *should* be fished during peak tidal flows. You may have to methodically work a large area before you find the route the fish prefer, and when they like to be there – but such featureless areas can, surprisingly, provide good fishing.

A perfect example of that is the Marin area herring spawns, which occur in relatively thin water, and the fish found at times on the flats between Point Chauncey and the San Rafael-Richmond Bridge. (See Cuanang's book for the details on that if you live in the Bay area.) And, many of the fish taken in Tillamook Bay come out of 10 to 12 feet of water.

Finally, wherever you roam, keep a weather eye out for those huge circular whirlpools known as eddies. They can trap weaker or wounded baitfish within their curling flow. That means more food concentrated in a smaller volume for the sturgeon. They'll often favor spots like this for the same reason you favor the refrigerator – more goodies to eat per cubic foot!

GEOGRAPHIC TOPOGRAPHY affects tidal flow. It may constrict the flow by funneling water into the narrow channel between two points. Naturally, that would increase the speed of the water. Naturally, that would stir up the bottom quite nicely. Good place for a lazy, hungry sturgeon, perhaps.

A single point jutting out into the bay will have a similar effect. At times, again for topographical reasons, a current can swing strongly into a smaller bay within the bay (a *cove*), follow this smaller bay's curving shoreline, then scoot on out the other side.

That may happen for only part of the tide. When it does, you may have some wonderful fishing within a few yards of shore in a few feet of water!

If this happens in the vicinity of a dock or a bunch of pilings, anchor just off to one side near the downcurrent end. Then flip something in the water back there. Pilings create added turbulence and damage an occasional baitfish. The downcurrent sides of bridge piers are very popular spots for the very same reasons.

And, sturgeon ain't stupid. Any fool knows that you use less energy staying alive if you get something between you and a hurricane. Not a bad analogy, actually, because if you stand behind the garage and hang a net out in a hundred mile an hour wind, a whole lot of things are going to fly into that bag.

(Remember this principle if you're a banker, as well. I've seen anglers on a fishing pier in San Francisco Bay wonder why all the fish were caught on one side in the morning and the other in the afternoon. It had nothing to do with the time of day, of course. It had to do with where the *downcurrent* side of the pilings was!)

Now to contradict everything I've said.

All that has to happen to re-arrange all of your hard-earned statistical data about a specific location is for the Corps of Engineers to come through and dredge a new shipping channel. The whole flow system of the bay will be altered.

Or, let's say, something less damaging occurs, like the eruption of a volcano.

I've fished the same Oregon trout stream for 38 years. Parts of that stream, holes or riffles I once regarded as legendary, are gone. The Corps didn't do it, the stream did it. A stream "meanders." It's a natural form. Snakes make a meander when they go for a walk. Rain meanders down a window pane.

It happens when the water, looking for the easiest path, unlike the Marines, takes the soft ground. That starts the wiggle. Then, because water flows faster on the outside of a curve than it does on the inside, sediment settles on one side and is dug out on the other. The corners slowly walk across the land, making wider and wider loops.

Any river or bay bottom changes naturally, as well. Things fill in and things are dug out. Sometimes, it's a cyclic thing, related to tidal range oscillations, or periodic

Sturgeon Fishing

(hundred year) flood levels. Sometimes the change just stays changed.

At times, distant natural cycles affect fishing. The cessation of cold water upwellings off the cost of Peru can dynamically alter baitfish populations on the West Coast of North America. Any change in numbers or arrival dates of baitfish will affect certain cyclical sturgeon concentrations.

All that tells us is that we have to keep an open mind about where (and when) the best spots are going to be next year. Those spots may change for any one reason, or any combination of them.

Since the principal behavior patterns remain the same, our data are still valid. Perhaps more valuable than ever. For, now we know what we're looking for.

When you know what you're looking for, you have a much better chance of finding it.

Jim Elliot with a stringer of Columbia River sturgeon.

Sturgeon Fishing Techniques

Chapter 6

Professional guides develop practices – trade secrets – that the occasional angler might never come across on his own. They also hear about tricks that work, and add these to their store of knowledge or lore.

PUT WHAT ON MY BAIT?

Who knows who first sprayed WD-40 brand lubricant on his bait and discovered that, sometimes, sturgeon will prefer the taste? Why would anyone even *think* to spray something like that on bait? But someone did . . . and sometimes it works.

Number 7 transmission fluid sometimes works, too. It may have something to do with the fact that the base for transmission fluid used to be whale oil (still is, in some primitive parts of the world). Maybe whatever synthetic base that now goes into the fluid tastes the same. Or better!

Or maybe it's just that some sturgeon are running low – starting to slip in "drive."

There is never any certainly as to what particular bait or bait-combination will appeal to sturgeon at any particular spot on any particular day. The general rule still applies, of course: "Match the hatch."

If smelt are running, bait with smelt. Ditto with anchovies, eel, and so forth. (If there is a shad run in, try that. Very large sturgeon love it.)

Sturgeon seem to prefer whatever is in greatest quantity on any particular day, and won't be interested in yesterday's menu at all. How that squares with transmission fluid and WD-40, we are at a loss to explain.

Sturgeon sometimes appear inordinately fond of night crawlers. No matter what your primary bait is, spearing a few worms on the end of the hook is a tactic worth trying.

And finally, another add-on to be used instead of (or in combination with) the various lubricants listed above is guide Gary Krum's favorite, Uncle Bob's brand salmon-egg oil.

WALKIN' YOUR BAIT DOWNSTREAM

For boat fishing in heavy currents like the Columbia (sometimes as deep as 70 feet), wire is better than monofilament. Wire is thinner, offering less resistance to the current. That means you can fish with less weight. And it doesn't stretch as plastic line does. You can set your rig with greater precision from a boat. When the sturgeon bites, you have a more direct connection. You can see the lighter bites better, and set the hook faster. (Less line stretch, less rod sweep required to drive the point home.)

Long casts are unnecessary from a boat—wire or mono—if the current is strong. You just drop your line over the stern, using 10 to 48 oz. of lead, depending upon the current. Pay-out line until the sinker strikes the bottom. Then pay out a couple more feet, trap the line with your thumb, lift the sinker and let the current "walk" it downstream, lowering the rod until the sinker strikes the bottom again. You can feel it. Repeat the process again and again until the sinker is as far downstream as you can get it—until the line is as nearly horizontal as possible. You'll know you've reached this point when you start to drag the

Sturgeon are nicknamed "alligators." In reality they are a shy fish very sensitive to vibrations and continually wiser to the ways of sturgeon fishermen. O.H.S. photo no. 67291.

sinker upstream instead of lifting it up from the bottom when you raise your rod tip.

Now is the time to flip the reel into gear and tigthen the drag. Don't forget. Otherwise, when you get your bite, you're going to haul back on the rod to set the hook, and find a nest of wire that A. T. & T. couldn't untangle.

Buoy oh buoy! One of the new trip-line anchor buoys. It slides up the line when you drop, remaining relatively close to your boat. When you're ready to hoist, just run back upcurrent and it works down the line, eventually raising the anchor by itself. *Photo by Larry Leonard.*

HOW MUCH WEIGHT?

The amount of lead you use depends on several factors, among them, whether you're fishing from boat or bank, and how much current there is.

If you're boat fishing, you'll rarely if ever use less than 4 oz. If you can keep less than that on the bottom, you're not in the current. Then you'll go home and say, "The sturgeon weren't biting today." Maybe so, maybe not. The problem was, you weren't fishing where the sturgeon were eating.

On the other hand, if the current is so strong that 48 oz. of lead on a wire line won't stay on the bottom, it's a good day to go home and tell fish stories. You're in trouble unless you are an expert boatman, or are with one. And even if you are, it's going to be murder trying to land a big fish. Certainly, maneuvering the boat for a long fight under such conditions would be next to impossible.

So for boats, the simple answer to the above question is: Between 4 oz. and 48 oz. And remember, the heavier the sinker, the more likely you are to lose it. Gary Krum, one of our resident experts, estimates that between 600-700 lbs. of sinkers leave his boat every year, never to return. "I've *paved* the mid-Columbia with lead!"

For bank fishermen, the answer is different. Don't use expensive lead sinkers, since you'll probably lose your weight every time you cast. Many bankers we know use worthless chunks of scrap metal—railraod spikes, etc. (There's a problem with spikes. They can take off an ear or give you a concussion. Certainly manufactured ball weights aren't as dangerous.)

SETTING THE HOOK

You're boat fishing, and the rod in your holder begins to nod. You wait for the next nod and then—Wham!—you set

Sturgeon Fishing

A fine setup. Northwest guide Gary Krum demonstrates the proper way to fish for sturgeon: sit back, relax and daydream. A 10-footer grabbed the rig (background) just after the author snapped this shot! *Photo by Larry Leonard.*

the hook. If you're right-handed, naturally you use your right arm to haul back on the rod. And thereby punch yourself in the nose.

Rule: Always use your *outboard* arm to set the hook. It takes a lot of force and a long pull — about three feet — to set the hook. If you use your inboard arm, you'll be trying to pull the rod across your body. No good: You'll exert less power, and incur the likelihood of hurting yourself.

If you're a bank fisherman, you may not have to set the hook. One angling method lets the sturgeon hook himself. With your weight out in the stream, fix your rod in its sand spike or other secure holder. Reel in until the rod is loaded: that is, until it is bent as far as it will go without dislodging the weight or the rod holder. As noted, when the sturgeon strikes he breaks the thin line holding the leader to the weight. The rod snaps up, and it's "Fish on!" Many bank fishermen attach a small bell to the tip of the rod, to announce the strike.

There are some exceptions to this method. A popular sturgeon spot is adjacent to Oregon City, Oregon. The Willamette River passes through a narrows just below the falls there. Anglers like to fish from the sidewalk along the east bank.

It is a strange location in some ways. The sidewalk railing is quite high above the river, so the cast to the water is a long one — almost straight down. It is unwise to fish this "hole" from a boat as large sinkers often snap loose and come flying at you like mortars.

Yet, people catch sturgeon here. And, the method used is similar to that we've described for working from a boat. A sliding sinker that allows you to see the bite.

If nothing else, this location proves the legendary durability of the fish. On the way up, they're banged time and time again against a rock, then a concrete wall. When released, they have almost as far to fall as those famous Hawaiian cliff divers. Maybe *as* far!

Somehow, many of them survive it all.

When you set the hook, according to some anglers, depends on the kind of bait you're using. If you're using worms or sand shrimp, try hitting the fish right away. With eels, smelt, herring and other baits, feed him a bit.

More than anything, the reason for this is the durability of the bait in question. Shrimp can be stripped off quickly unless they're well wound on the hook with thread. You can't wind worms on the hook with thread.

LINE VS. WIRE

Since 30 lb. test monofilament is sufficient to land any legal sturgeon (except in California, where they allow females greater than six feet to be killed), why go to the extra expense of 100 lb. test wire? A few reasons: wire lasts much longer. When fishing from a boat, it offers less resistance to the water and doesn't stretch, as mono does, so you can feel the bite. (And the reason for 100 lb. test instead of more common 60 lb. is that the former is easier on roller guides, and is less likely to break if it gets a kink.)

Monofilament is more practical for bank fishing, because if you're using the newer bent-rod technique, you don't need to feel the bite. The sturgeon hooks himself, as we said above. You know about it when your pole snaps up and your reel gets hot. (You don't completely "lock" down the drag when banking, as you do on a boat, or you'll lose your rig. The whole thing, not just "hook, line and sinker." Unless you happen to be holding on for dear life at the time of the strike. If not, you soon will be!) Also, mono is cheaper, and bankers lose more rigs.

WHERE THE HECK ARE THEY?

The eternal question. All too often the answer seems to

Fish on! Legendary angler Lee Tomerlin has pulled the string on a keeper. *Photo by Larry Leonard.*

An *hors d'oeuvre!* Fish under 5 feet in length can be handled easily. It doesn't hurt to wear gloves when you're doing it, though. *Photo by Larry Leonard.*

One for the table. Except for the rattlesnake diamonds on the side, they do look like sharks, don't they? *Photo by Larry Leonard.*

A throwback. Gary Krum prepares to release the author's legal, but smaller, sturgeon. (Leonard's baby is due in three months.) *Photo by Lee Tomerlin.*

be, "Wherever the heck I *ain't!*" You frequently see a "hog line," with everyone using the same bait and rigs, but only a few will see any action. For them, it's just bite-bite-bite, hour after hour. Everybody else in the line gets skunked. Luck seems to have as much to do with it as skill.

But skill *can* improve your chances to get lucky! We've talked about the importance of a chart recorder, if you're boat fishing. Look for side-slopes and down-slopes. If you're a banker, look for narrow channels, river islands, bars . . . anywhere there's roiling water on the bottom, or the water is compressed (and therefore running faster). That's where the bottom food collects, and food is where you'll find the sturgeon. The only time sturgeon don't eat is when they sleep. And sturgeon don't sleep.

(Fore more detail on this, reread chapter five.)

REELING HIM IN

There's a particular way to hold the rod when you have a sturgeon on. It's a method that avoids two particularly unfortunate consequences: 1) losing your rod, and 2) becoming a soprano.

Let us say you have set the hook. Now it is fun time. If he's a monster and is going to give you a fight, you have loosened the drag slightly. If he's not so big, you've left the drag tight. Either way, here's how to hold the rod while reeling:

Place the butt of the rod against the front of your left thigh where it joins your torso. (Do *not* trap it between your thighs. You could have *one-thousand pounds of fighting fish* on the other end!).

Hold the rod just ahead of the reel with your left hand, so that the palm of your hand and wrist hold the reel upright. This way it won't wobble back and forth as you work the reel with your right hand.

Simple!

A SHORT SERMON

Hook all the sturgeon you want. The roofs of their mouths are solid gristle, very tough, and it won't hurt them. You both get some wonderful exercise. Take pictures. But don't kill them just to fill your freezer. If all you want is meat, go to the market. It's cheaper. Frozen fish should be consumed within six months, tops, and one sturgeon represents a *lot* of fish. It takes a long time to eat four-dozen cans of smoked sturgeon. Wait until you're down to the last few cans before you take another. In other words, have your fun, but unless you really need him, turn him loose to help assure a strong sturgeon fishery for yourself in years to come.

If you think this message is pessimistic, friend, consider this: Unless the regs have changed while this book was going to press, there is no waterway left in Idaho where it is legal to keep sturgeon. It is all catch-and-release now. Fish three to six feet long have just about disappeared from the Snake River, which was once the most abundant source of sturgeon in the West. It can happen, *and may be happening now,* in California, Oregon, Washington, and British Columbia as well.

Young sturgeon less than a year old. *Oregon Department of Fish and Wildlife photo*

How to Take Your Sturgeon Apart

Chapter 7

It's time to clean your catch, unless you're taking him to a canner to do it. Don't clean him on the dock without permission of the dock owner or manager. And, if you have permission, clean up your mess. If it isn't a long drive, the fish will keep until you get home.

The first step is to revive your wife and tell her that you were only kidding; you'll do it. If she complains that it's *still* too ugly to eat, explain that medical researchers report that the oil of white-meat fish is very healthy (it is), and will help her lose weight. (It won't. Lie.)

(By the way, the author knows the above paragraph is sexist. Tough. This is a book for fisher*men*. Fisherpersons can read this one or write their own.)

The second step is to decide how thorough you want to be, that is, how much of the meat you want to recover. Since most people are interested only in the white meat — the red has a very strong taste, but your cat will love it — Gary Krum of Oregon Fishing Adventures employs a simple procedure.

SIMPLE CLEANING

Immediately after catching, run a rope through one

gillcover and out the mouth. Then slit one of the gills. Tie the fish off and put it back in the water to bleed.

When you've arrived at your cleaning station, do as follows:

Remove the diamond-shaped body plates in strips by cutting about 1/4 inch beneath the skin. Draw them forward, tail-to-head.

Over the top. Remove the back spines in a strip.

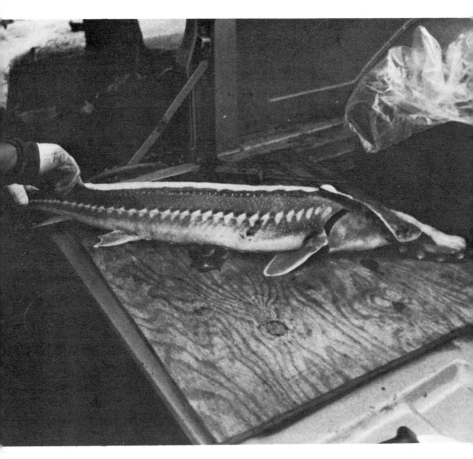

Cut away the dorsal, pelvic and anal fins.

To remove the "notocord" (the soft tube inside the backbone) cut around the base of the tail until you see the

Down the side. Fillet between the interior carcass and the meat.

And, the meat goes on. Repeat the cut down the other side.

white cartilage, but don't cut it. Twist the tail until the cartilage cracks; then draw it back from the body. The
notocord will come with it.

Now skin the fish by drawing the remaining strips off,
head-to-tail.

Cut off the head behind the gills, remove the rest of the
skin and gut the fish. He's ready now to be cut into steaks,
fillets, chunks or however you wish.

There's a quicker method, if you're one of those long-
time coastal anglers and have filleted your share of bottom-
fish. Simply run the knife along the notocord—without cutting it, of course—and trim the meat away from the inner
cavity. Then make a notch at the tail end and, holding the
knife at a nearly flat, downward angle, swing and sway the
meat from the skin the same way you would a ling cod's

Trim off the red meat and you're ready to go.

How to Take Your Sturgeon Apart

Bottoms up. Trim along the belly of the slab.

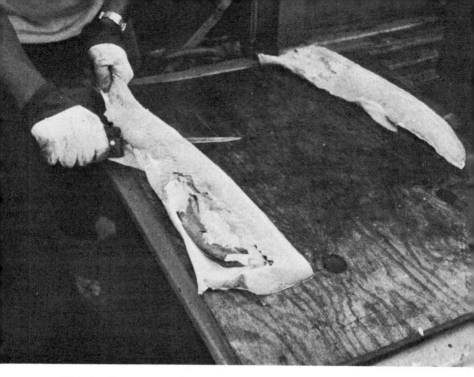

Skin it. Cut a crosswise notch at the back, hold the strip with one hand and work the knife up toward the front.

Trim it. Cut away everything but the best white meat. You're done. *Series photos by Larry Leonard.*

How to Take Your Sturgeon Apart

George Burdick with sturgeon caught in the Klamath River.

No one knows how many pounds this sturgeon caught by Cascade Locks weighs. *Oregon Historical Society photo no. 38600.*

Guess Who's Coming to Dinner?

Chapter 8

Okay, you've caught the critter. You can't cook it like a trout unless you buy a six-foot frying pan, right? So you have two options at least: Take him to a commercial canner or take him home. Or a combination of the two (the author's preference): Have the canner cut some steaks out of the fillets before he cans the rest, half of which he smokes. There are greater and lesser canners; before you go fishing, ask someone who knows.

In all cases below, "sturgeon" refers to the white meat. The red meat has a stronger flavor than most people prefer; always trim it and cartilage away during preparation.

Abe Cuanang says that sturgeon cooked the same day it's caught tends to be tough. He suggests it be stored in the refrigerator two or three days before eating.

The first great thrill of your sturgeon expedition was getting him in the boat or ashore. Now for the second great thrill: Getting him inside *you!*

Everyone has a favorite recipe or variation. Doubtless you will develop your own. In the meantime, here are some of the preferences enjoyed by our various sources.

STURGEON IN MORNAY SAUCE

Sauté fish fillets in a little butter.

Make cheese sauce (flour, water, butter, salt, pepper; heat and blend, melt cheese in).

Add one can of shrimp to sauce and heat through.

Put sautéed fillets into oven dish. Cover with sauce, sprinkle seedless grapes on top and bake in 350-degree oven for five to ten minutes. (It's easy to overcook any fish, so keep an eye on it. If it's tender when you poke it with a fork, it's done.)

DEEP FRIED STURGEON

Dip fillets in batter of egg and milk.

Then dip in mixture of one-half Jiff Corn Meal and one-half flour, plus salt and pepper.

Fry in deep fryer or pan with a half-inch of hot oil.

BAKED STURGEON

Dip fillets in mixture of (Half?) cup of milk and 2 tsp. salt.

Roll fish in fine dry bread crumbs.

Place an oiled, shallow baking pan and drizzle each piece lightly with oil.

Bake at 500 degrees uncovered for ten to 15 minutes. Do not add water or turn fillets.

STURGEON AND ALMONDS

1/2 cup butter	2 T. dried dill seed
2/3 cup silvered almonds	1/4 tsp. salt
1/4 cup dry white wine or sherry	1/4 tsp. pepper
1/4 cup lemon juice	1 lb. sturgeon

Sauté almonds in butter; remove almonds and save.
Mix wine, juice and seasonings.
Place fillets in sauce and spoon sauce over.
Cover and cook six to eight minutes.
Garnish with almonds and serve covered with sauce.

STURGEON CASSEROLE

2 lbs. sturgeon
1 lb. fresh mushrooms; sauté in 2 T. butter.
  Mix together:
2 cans creamed celery soup (undiluted)

1/3 can parmesan cheese	2 T. sherry
1 T. parsley	1/2 tsp. dry crushed basil

1 pkg. shrimp

Layer bottom of baking dish with fish. Sprinkle with salt, pepper, paprika, 2 T. flour, mushrooms, then sauce.
Sprinkle top with crumbs.
Bake 30 minutes at 375 degrees.
Let stand for ten minutes, then cut and serve.

All of the above recipes were submitted by Gary Krum of Oregon Fishing Adventures

STARK STREET STURGEON

7 oz. sturgeon	**1½4 T. cracked peppercorns**

6 to 8 fresh basil leaves (coarsely chopped)

1 T. oil	**Flour**	**1 T. butter**
1 T. prepared mustard	**2 T. water as needed**	

Season sturgeon with salt and pepper, dust with flour. Heat pan to medium-high and add oil.

When hot, add sturgeon. Cook both sides until lightly browned.

Remove, wipe pan clean. Add butter, basil, pepper and mustard.

Cook for 20 to 30 seconds. Add water and stir; do not cook. If sauce is not homogenous, add a touch more water.

Pour sauce over sturgeon, garnish with basil leaves.

STURGEON FOR SUSIE

7 oz. sturgeon	**1 oz. oil**	**1 T. butter**

1 T. real bacon bits, chopped fine

2 oranges, juice of one and peeled sections of other

1 T. toasted sliced almonds

1 pinch fresh chopped parsley

Salt and pepper to taste

Cut sturgeon into 2 oz. medallions. Dust in flour.

Saute in oil medium to high heat until cooked through and slightly brown both sides.

Remove sturgeon from pan, pour off excess fat, add bacon bits plus 1 T. butter. Cook until hot, slightly brown.

Quickly add orange juice, almonds, orange sections and parsley.

Saute until all ingredients are hot. Add a touch of whole butter if necessary. Do not overcook.

Spoon mixture on top of sturgeon and serve immediately.

Guess Who's Coming to Dinner?

The last two recipes are from Marcel Lahsene, head chef at Jake's Famous Crawfish in Portland, Oregon, as published in the Fall '85 issue of Seafood Leader Magazine.

BAKED STURGEON (By Bonny Almeida)

Cut sturgeon into 3/4 inch steaks.
Place in oven dish and baste liberally with melted butter.
Cover with generous coating of Progresso brand Italian style bread crumbs.
Bake in preheated 350 degree oven for 10 to 15 minutes, until tender when pierced with a fork.

STURGEON SCHNITZEL (By Bonny Almeida)

Sauce:

1 large chopped onion	1/2 cup Chablis
2 oz. brandy	1 tsp. garlic powder
1 tsp. coarse-ground black pepper	2 oz. soy sauce
1/2 tsp. salt	1 T. paprika
4 oz. olive oil	

Liquefy all ingredients in blender. Heat to boil in sauce pan; then turn down to simmer for 10 minutes, stirring constantly with flat-edged wooden spoon.
Mix together 2 T. flour with 3/4 cup water and stir into sauce. Continue stirring until sauce is desired thickness.
Dust both sides of 1/4 inch sturgeon fillets with salt, pepper and garlic powder.
Beat enough eggs to cover fish. Mix in salt, pepper and garlic powder to taste.
Dip fish into egg mixture, dredge through flour mix, and fry in cast-iron pan with hot olive oil. Don't over-fry!
Serve fried fillets immediately after covering with sauce.

STURGEON JERKY (By Steve Dypvik)

Cut sturgeon into 1/8 inch strips, *with grain.*

Marinade:
1 cup soy sauce
4 T. granulated sugar
1 tsp. black pepper

Mix ingredients into large frying pan at high heat until bubbling.

Let coool slightly and add sturgeon strips.

Marinate about 20 minutes, stirring to assure even coating.

Place strips on oven racks to cool (line bottom of oven with aluminum foil to catch drips).

Sprinkle fish with ground black pepper, covering completely.

Store jerky in airtight containers at room temperature.

FAST-FRIED STURGEON (By Simone Herault)

Cut sturgeon into 1/2 inch steaks.

Cover both sides with Progresso brand Italian style bread crumbs.

Fry in butter three to five minutes each side.

HOME "SMOKED" STURGEON (By Bonny Almeida)

Marinade:

1 gal. water	**3/4 cup salt**
1 sliced lemon	**1 cup soy sauce**
6 cloves crushed garlic	**6 bay leaves**
1 T. coarse pepper	**2 T. paprika**
3 oz. olive oil	**1 cup dark brown sugar**

Mix the above and stir well.

Cut sturgeon into thin, 10-inch strips; marinate 24 hours.

Dry strips for an hour and cover with brown sugar; then sprinkle with soy sauce.

Place fish on trays covered with aluminum foil.

Bake five to six hours in 350 degree oven until done.

The above five recipes are based on some that appeared in Abe Cuanang's book, San Francisco Bay Sturgeon.

BRAISED STURGEON WITH GARLIC RASPBERRY SAUCE

2 cups fresh raspberries   1/4 cup water

Place berries in saucepan with water, bring to simmer over medium-low heat; cook until soft purée stage, stirring occasionally. Sieve through mesh strainer to remove seeds. Set aside.

5 T. clarified butter	**4 6-oz. fresh sturgeon fillets**
Salt and white pepper to taste	
Juice from 1/2 lemon	**6 T. Madeira, divided**
1 tsp. minced garlic	**1/2 tsp. minced shallots**
2 T. heavy cream	**Fresh raspberries for garnish**

Melt butter in sauté pan, place fillets in pan, season lightly with salt and pepper.

Brown fillets on both sides over medium-high heat; sauté until they are about half-cooked.

Pour lemon juice over fillets.

Deglaze pan with Madeira, remove from heat, transfer fillets to oven dish. Keep warm in 300 degree oven. They will finish cooking while sauce is made.

Put sauté pan back on heat, add minced garlic and shallots, shake pan to agitate contents just until garlic becomes slightly browned.

Add 2 T. Madeira, stir to deglaze pan and mix thoroughly.

Add raspberry purée, cook gently for two to three minutes to slightly reduce mixture and marry flavors.

Stir in heavy cream, heat just until mixture is warmed and blended.

Remove fillets from oven, lace raspberry sauce over fish, garnish each with a few raspberries. Serve immediately.

The above recipe was sent to the author, photocopied from an unidentified publication. Its creator was not named in the article.

MRS. REIBER'S HUSBAND'S SMOKED STURGEON

Begin with a sturgeon that is between 38 and 46 inches in length.

Fillet the fish.

Put 1½ gallons of water in a bucket.

Mix in:

Two cups of rock salt (do NOT use table salt).
1½ cups brown sugar.
Five to six tablespoons of soy sauce.
Three tablespoons of garlic salt or powder.

Guess Who's Coming to Dinner?

Brine the critter for four hours, then stick a garden hose down in the bucket and give it a good flushing to get rid of all the surface salt. Air dry the fillets in a cool place overnight. Next sprinkle the fillets with garlic salt, pepper and lemon. Put them in a heavy, but cool, smoke for 7-8 hours. Remove the fillets (or chunks) from the smoker and put them on a tray in your oven. Cook them at 300 degrees for twenty minutes. Remove from the oven and give them a slow cool.

The key to this process is doing the cooking in the **oven** instead of in the smoker.

(**Author's Note:** Mrs. Reiber owns the Garibaldi Marina on Tillamook Bay in Oregon. I have eaten her husband's smoked sturgeon, and as a result hope that when I reach Heaven, Jerry is the chef there.)

VITAL NOTICE

It is absolutely imperative to the success of all of the recipes presented here, that whenever you serve them you invite the author to dinner. We cannot otherwise be held responsible for whether or not they come out tasting as good as they should!

ATTENTION FISHERMAN

Sturgeon Have Been Tagged in the Columbia & Willamette Rivers. In Some Cases Two Different Types of Tags are on a Fish.

IF YOU CATCH A TAGGED FISH & IT'S **NOT** OF LEGAL SIZE (3'-6'), **PLEASE DO NOT REMOVE TAG!** Please record:

1. Tag Number & Color
2. Date and Location Caught
3. Length & Weight (if possible)

4. RETURN THE FISH TO RIVER
5. Return Information to Department

IF THE TAGGED FISH **IS** OF LEGAL SIZE & YOU WISH TO KEEP IT, PLEASE RETURN THE TAG WITH THE ABOVE INFORMATION TO:

OREGON DEPT. OF FISH AND WILDLIFE
P. O. Box 59
Portland, OR 97208

WASHINGTON DEPT. OF FISHERIES
PO Box 999 MS S-13
Battle Ground WA 98604

Columbia River Upstream to Bonneville Dam

Thousands of sturgeon migrate into the Columbia from the ocean in spring to feed & spawn. Look for holes, ask at bait shops, look for anchored boats.

DODSON AREA

WASHINGTON

scale of miles

0 2 4

Beacon Rock

channel markers

sound beach light "83"

Pierce Island
Ives Island
Hamilton Island
Bradford Island

COLUMBIA RIVER

Covert's Landing

Dodson

exit 35

OREGON

84

Bonneville Dam

11 10 9 8 7 6 5 4 3 2 1

Covert's Landing near Dodson has bait, tackle and sturgeon information plus paved ramp, moorage, gas and camping. Salmon and shad information, also. Dodson area sturgeon fishing map courtesy of Ken Covert. Phone (503) 374-8577.

Hood River

Bradford Island

Bonneville

Dodson

Rooster Rock

WASHINGTON River

Camas

Columbia

Vancouver

5

Portland

84

Longview

Kelso

Rainier

Goble

Columbia City

St. Helens

Sauvie Island

OREGON

Willamette River to falls at Oregon City offers good fishing holes.

Skamokawa

Wauna

4

30

Svensen

Astoria

Gray's Bay

101

101

Willapa Bay

PACIFIC OCEAN

Most Productive Sturgeon Fishing Areas

1 100-foot hole—at the edge of the back-eddy.
2 50- to 60-foot hole—out from the old piling.
3 60- to 90-foot hole—out from Horsetail Falls.
4 35- to 50-foot Washington side of channel.
5 50- to 60-foot—off sand beach.
6 80- to 100-foot—edge of back-eddy.
7 80- to 100-foot—out from old pilings.
8 30- to 50-foot—edge of back-eddy
9, 10, 11 big fish, fast current, not recommended for amateurs.

This 1500-pound white sturgeon was caught in the Snake River near Payette, Idaho, in the late 1800's. O.H.S. photo no. 34255.